最新時事テーマ収録
Readings at the **EXAM STANDARD** level

Cutting Edge

ナビブック 付

速読トレーニング
文構造解説
重要語句
語句確認ドリル

Blue

本書は、入試標準レベルの英文読解力を段階的に養成で
きるように編集されています。

英文素材について

① 新しい素材で、「読む価値がある英文」であること
② 文系・理系のテーマのバランスを取ること
③ 難易度にバラつきがでないこと

を基準に厳選しました。そうして選ばれた英文を、段階的に有名私大・国公
立二次レベルの読解力を養成できるように、易〜難へ配列しています。

設問について

「構文・語彙」など、入試の設問になりやすい部分と、内容理解のポイント
となる部分に、英文の流れに沿って設問を配置しています。設問をはじめか
ら解いていくことで、内容が理解できる構成になっています。

語彙について

「Navi Book」では、英文内の重要語句をレベル別にほぼ全て網羅してお
り、覚えるべき語句とそうでないものが一目瞭然になっています。また「英
単語」→「日本語の意味」の順で読み上げた音声もあるので、より効果的な
単語学習ができるようになっています。さらに、「Navi Book」の巻末には定
着を図るために実際の入試問題で構成された「**語句確認ドリル**」を収録してい
ます。英文の中で触れた語彙を確実に覚えることが語彙力増強への最短距離
です。入試頻出のものばかりですので、何度も繰り返し確認してください。

背景情報について

新たな英文を読む際、その英文の中で扱われている内容についての背景知
識があると、英文は格段に理解しやすくなります。本書では、全課に「**テーマ
解説**」を、また時事用語などには「**用語解説**」を用意しました。「典型的な頻
出英文テーマ」や時事的な用語など、英文に関する背景情報に目を通してお
くだけでも受験には非常に有効です。

【本書の設問について】

▶ 設問指示文右端の大学名は、出題校で実際に出題された問題です。その他の設問は、
出題傾向、難易度、記述・客観のバランスに合わせて作成されたオリジナル問題です。

CONTENTS

共通テスト ⇒ 国公立二次・有名私大レベル

Part 1

Chapter 1	4	「教育と疾病」	東京理科大
Chapter 2	6	「最後のメッセージ」	明治学院大
Chapter 3	8	「目の大きさと脳の関係」	岡山大
Chapter 4	10	「液体燃料問題」	鹿児島大

Part 2

Chapter 5	12	「貴重な教訓」	関西学院大
Chapter 6	14	「コーク VS ペプシ」	宮城大
Chapter 7	16	「動物の社会的距離」	北里大
Chapter 8	18	「睡眠の役割」	三重大

Part 3

Chapter 9	20	「口論と真実」	愛知教育大
Chapter 10	22	「オーガニック」	名古屋市立大
Chapter 11	26	「自動運転車」	法政大
Chapter 12	28	「AI と仕事」	滋賀県立大

国公立二次・有名私大レベル

Part 4

Chapter 13	32	「行動の背景」	弘前大
Chapter 14	34	「災害と温暖化」	広島大
Chapter 15	36	「ビッグデータ」	法政大
Chapter 16	38	「『事実』なるもの」	岩手大

Part 5

| Chapter 17 | 40 | 「ハビタブルゾーン」 | 西南学院大 |
| Chapter 18 | 44 | 「確証バイアス」 | 北海道大 |

テーマ解説・用語解説　49

語　数 ： 381 語
出題校 ： 東京理科大

For the first time in history, a major disease might soon be eliminated without the ⊕1-1
use of drugs. The Carter Center, an organization run by former US President Jimmy
Carter, has predicted that the Guinea worm★ disease will be the first parasitic disease
to be (1)eradicated and the first disease to be (1)eradicated without the use of vaccines
or medical treatment. The Guinea worm is (2)a parasite, which is an organism or
creature that lives on or in another organism or creature. People get Guinea worm
disease by drinking dirty, contaminated water. After drinking contaminated water, the
worms grow in the body for about a year. Once they have grown, they emerge slowly
from the body often around the foot area. It can take weeks for the worm to fully
emerge. And during this time, the victim is in great pain, making it almost impossible
for the victim to work, move around or go about their lives.

But the Guinea worm can now only be found in a few African countries, thanks to ⊕1-2
a 22-year fight against the disease led by the Carter Center. Carter was moved when
he saw its victims in Africa. "It was a horrible disease, almost indescribably bad. It
was an ancient disease and it didn't seem to have any solution. (3)It was almost an
impossible problem, so that's why we decided to try to solve it."

The strategy to eliminate this disease has been consistent: (4)public education. ⊕1-3
Previously, villagers thought the disease came from witchcraft, or from eating bad
meat. (　5　), now they know that it comes from the ponds, where they get their
drinking water. This disease has tormented villagers for thousands of years and it will
soon be eliminated by educating the villagers and teaching them to use very simple
water filters. In 1986, there were an estimated 3.5 million cases of Guinea worm in
21 countries in Africa and Asia. In 2012, there were only 512 documented cases in
four countries in sub-Saharan Africa. The Carter Center, along with the US chemical
company Dupont, developed a fine cloth filter which was effective and could be made
and distributed cheaply. (6)By filtering all the village drinking water through these fine
cloths, the villagers were able to stop the worms from entering the human body.

　　★　Guinea worm「ギニア虫」

1 下線部 (1) の語に文脈上最も近い意味のものを 1 つ選びなさい。

① gotten rid of　　② spread　　③ found out　　④ investigated

2 下線部 (2) を 20 字以上 30 字以内の日本語で説明しなさい。

3 下線部 (3) を、文頭の It の内容を明らかにして日本語にしなさい。

4 下線部 (4) の具体的な内容を 40 字以内の日本語で説明しなさい。

5 空所 (5) に入る最も適切な語を 1 つ選びなさい。　　　　　(東京理科大)

① However　　② Moreover　　③ Otherwise　　④ Thus

6 下線部 (6) を日本語にしなさい。　　　　　(東京理科大・改)

7 本文の内容に一致するものを 1 つ選びなさい。　　　　　(東京理科大)

① The Carter Center cured the African disease by itself.

② The Guinea worms can dissolve in the body for weeks.

③ 512 cases of Guinea worm were prevented in 21 countries in 2012.

④ The Guinea worm disease was beaten by simple tools.

⑤ Water filters and education are irrelevant for disease control.

語　数：518 語
出題校 ： 明治学院大

When I married my husband, six years ago, he already had four small children from his previous marriage. I became their stepmother, and watched them become young teenagers. Although they lived primarily with their mother, they spent a lot of time with us as well. Over the years, we all learned to adjust. We enjoyed vacations together, ate family meals, worked on homework, played baseball, rented videos. However, (1)I continued to feel somewhat like an outsider. Since I had no children of my own, my experience of parenting was limited to my husband's four, and often I felt sad because I would never know the special bond that exists between a parent and a child.

When the children moved to a town that was a five-hour drive away, my husband was understandably upset. We promptly set up an e-mail and chat-line service. (2)This technology, combined with the telephone, would enable us to reach the children on a daily basis by sending frequent notes and messages, and even chatting together when we were all on-line.

Ironically, these modern tools of communication can also be (3)tools of alienation, making us feel so out of touch, so much more in need of real human contact. If a computer message came addressed to "Dad", I'd feel forgotten and neglected. If my name appeared along with his, it would brighten my day and make me feel like I was part of (4)their family unit after all. Yet always there was some distance to be crossed, not just over the telephone wires.

Late one evening, as my husband slept in front of the television and I was catching up on my e-mail, an "instant message" appeared on the screen. It was from Margo, my oldest step-daughter, also up late and sitting in front of her computer five hours away. As usual, we sent several messages back and forth, exchanging the latest news. (5)When we would "chat" like that, she wouldn't necessarily know if it was me or her dad operating the keyboard — that is unless she asked. That night she didn't ask and I didn't identify myself either. After hearing the latest volleyball scores, the details about an upcoming dance at her school, and a history project she was working on, I commented that it was late and I should get to sleep. Her return message read, "Okay, talk to you later! Love you!"

As I read this message, a wave of sadness ran through me, as (6)I realized that she must have thought she was writing to her father the whole time. She and I would never have openly exchanged such words of affection. Feeling guilty for not clarifying, yet not wanting to embarrass her, I simply responded, "I love you too! Have a good sleep!"

I thought again of their family circle, that self-contained, private space where I was an outsider. I felt again the sharp ache of emptiness and otherness. Then, just as I was ³⁵ about to log off, Margo's final message appeared. It read, "Tell Dad good night for me too." With tear-filled, blurry eyes, I turned the computer off.

❶ 筆者が下線部 (1) のように感じていた理由を 40 字以内の日本語で説明しなさい。

❷ 下線部 (2) とほぼ同じ意味になるように、次の英文の空所に適語を入れなさい。

By ₁.(   ) this technology together with the telephone, we would

₂.(   ) ₃.(   ) ₄.(   ) reach the children every day.

❸ 下線部 (3) の具体的内容を簡潔な日本語で説明しなさい。

_____

_____

❹ 下線部 (4) と同意の表現を本文中から抜き出しなさい。

_____

❺ 下線部 (5) を日本語にしなさい。

_____

_____

_____

❻ 下線部 (6) のように考えた根拠を簡潔な日本語で説明しなさい。

_____

❼ 内容に一致するものを 2 つ選びなさい。   (明治学院大)

① The children spent most of their time living with the writer's wife.

② The writer always felt like a part of the inner family circle.

③ The writer regretted not being able to experience genuine parental feelings.

④ The writer used computer technology to communicate with the children.

⑤ The writer especially liked messages that were addressed to "Dad".

⑥ Margo always knew who was writing messages to her.

⑦ Margo and the writer exchanged information about the father's hobbies.

⑧ After reading Margo's final words, the writer cried and turned off the computer sadly.

3

語　数 ： 378 語
出題校 ： 岡山大

(1)A study suggests that people who live at higher latitudes* have larger eyes and 🔊 1-18
more ability in their brains to deal with visual information compared with those living
nearer the equator*. Researchers measured the brain volumes and eye sizes of 55 skulls
kept at the Oxford University Museum of Natural History dating from the 19th century.
5 The skulls represented 12 different populations from around the world, including native
people from England, Australia, China, Kenya, Micronesia and Scandinavia.

"As you move away from the equator, there's less and less light available, so 🔊 1-19
humans have had to evolve bigger and bigger eyes," said (2)Ellie Pearce, a graduate
student from Oxford University and the lead author on the study. "Their brains also
10 need to be bigger to deal with the extra visual input. Having bigger brains doesn't
mean that higher-latitude humans are (A); it just means they need bigger brains to
be able to see well where they live." This suggests that someone from Greenland and
someone from Kenya will have the same ability to detect detail, but the person from
the higher latitude needs more brainpower and bigger eyes to deal with the lower light
15 levels.

Professor Robin Dunbar, also from Oxford University and a co-author of the 🔊 1-20
study, said that people whose ancestors lived within the Arctic Circle* have eyeballs
20% bigger than people whose ancestors lived near the equator. They have an
associated increase in the size of the visual part of the brain, which previous studies
20 have shown matches with the size of the eyeball. Brain volume increases with latitude:
people living at high latitudes north and south of the equator have bigger brains than
people living near the equator.

The results, published in the journal *Biology Letters*, showed that the biggest brains, 🔊 1-21
averaging 1,484 milliliters, were from Scandinavia, while the smallest brains, around
25 1,200 milliliters, came from Micronesia. The average eye size was 27 milliliters in
Scandinavia and 22 milliliters in Micronesia. Professor Dunbar concluded that the
increase in brain volume must have evolved relatively recently in human history. He
added, "It's only within the last 10,000 years or so that modern humans have occupied
all latitudes right up to the Arctic Circle. So, (3)this is probably (4)a development that's
30 happened within the last 10,000 years."

＊ latitude「緯度」 equator「赤道」 Arctic Circle「北極圏」

1 下線部（1）に関し、以下の質問に日本語で答えなさい。 (岡山大・改)

（1） この研究が示していることを説明しなさい。

_____

_____

（2） 研究者たちはどのようにしてデータを得たか、説明しなさい。

_____

_____

2 下線部（2）の Ellie Pearce の意見を、日本語で簡単にまとめなさい。 (岡山大)

_____

_____

3 文脈から判断して、（A）に入る最も適切なものを 1 つ選びなさい。

① less intelligent   ② bigger   ③ smarter   ④ better looking

4 下線部（3）this が指しているものを 1 つ選びなさい。

① The study of the brain volume and eye size.
② The increase in brain volume.
③ The increase in eye size in Micronesia.
④ Modern humans occupation of all latitudes.

5 下線部（4）のように言える理由を、本文に即して日本語で説明しなさい。

_____

_____

6 本文の内容と一致するものを 1 つずつ選びなさい。

（1） Ellie Pearce's study suggests that ...
① people living at higher latitudes have larger eyes than those living at lower latitudes, but there is no big difference between them in the size of brains.
② the brains as well as the eyes of the people living in Scandinavia are bigger than those of the people living in Kenya.
③ the farther from the equator people live, the larger eyes and the greater power of vision they have.

（2） Professor Robin Dunbar said that ...
① people's eye sizes have more to do with where they have lived recently than with where their ancestors lived.
② bigger size of brains of Scandinavian people mean that their ancestors began to live near the Arctic Circle more than 10,000 years ago.
③ as modern humans spread to higher latitudes, people living there have acquired larger visual part of the brain and bigger eyeballs.

語　数：424 語
出題校：鹿児島大

I have a friend who likes to barbecue on his back deck. He puts charcoal in the   🔊 1-26
grill, squirts★ some lighter fluid★ on the charcoal, and throws a match on it. The
lighter fluid goes "BOOM," but somehow his charcoal never starts burning. So he
squirts more lighter fluid, lights another match, and watches it blow up again while
his wife and I make fun of him. He makes frequent trips to the store for more lighter
fluid. (1)One day his wife commented, "Charlie's charcoal grill runs on lighter
fluid."

In a way, muscle is like that grill. Muscle burns both fat and sugar: the sugar   🔊 1-27
burns instantly like lighter fluid, yielding only a small amount of energy, but the fat
continues to burn for a long, long time, like charcoal (A). You get lots more
calories, or energy, from a fat molecule★ than you do from a sugar molecule. When
you're playing active sports you may run out of sugar; you never run out of fat.

We now know that even people who are starving never, never, never (B) all of   🔊 1-28
their body fat. This may surprise you, since starving or anorexic★ people look so
emaciated★, but there is fat even on the bodies of people who weigh only seventy-five
pounds. They look like skeletons when they die because they lose so much muscle,
but autopsies★ show that they still have ten or fifteen pounds of fat hidden inside.
(2)These people do not, in fact, starve to death.

Nobody in the history of the earth has ever actually starved to death. (3)At some   🔊 1-29
point during starvation, as the body runs out of glucose★ it starts using protein for
fuel. In the process of burning protein, it taps★ the immune system antibodies★, which
are proteins. Starving people become highly susceptible★ to bacteria and viruses;
they die of infectious diseases precipitated★ by lack of protein in their bodies.

Like starving people, those who are very fit occasionally have (4)lighter-fluid   🔊 1-30
problems. During long, rigorous sports events their muscles run out of sugar. (5)When
that happens, their energy drops abruptly★ because the burning of fat, triggered by
sugar's spark, has ceased. Athletes think they run out of energy because their sugar
has run out, but in reality, they have plenty of "fat energy" left (C). They constantly
look for ways to store more sugar in their muscles, mistakenly thinking that sugar is
their primary fuel. But it is only the starter fluid; fat is the primary fuel.

★ squirt「吹きかける」　lighter fluid「液体燃料」　molecule「分子」　anorexic「拒食症の」　emaciated「やせ衰えた」
autopsy「解剖」　glucose「ブドウ糖」　tap「資源として活用する」　immune system antibody「免疫系の抗体」
susceptible「影響されやすい」　precipitate「突然引き起こす」　abruptly「突然、不意に」

1 彼の妻（his wife）はなぜ下線部（1）のように言ったのか。理由を日本語で説明しなさい。 （鹿児島大）

2 （A）～（C）に入れるのに最も適切なものを1つずつ選びなさい。 （鹿児島大）

(A) ① because sugar does not need charcoal ② even if it does not get started

③ once it gets started ④ only when it burns easily

(B) ① make up ② put out ③ take in ④ use up

(C) ① and know many ways to draw from it ② and try to find ways to avoid it

③ but cannot survive without it ④ but no way to draw from it

3 下線部（2）のような状況が生じる医学的理由を60字以内の日本語で説明しなさい。 （鹿児島大）

4 下線部（3）を it の意味がはっきりわかるようにして日本語にしなさい。 （鹿児島大）

5 下線部（4）の説明としてふさわしいものを1つ選びなさい。

① People try hard to make up for the loss of sugar while they really need glucose.

② People run out of fat because they take in too much sugar.

③ People burn out sugar though they still have enough fat.

④ People suffer from lack of fat when they really need it.

6 下線部（5）を that の意味がはっきりわかるようにして日本語にしなさい。 （鹿児島大）

7 fat と sugar について本文の内容と一致するものを1つ選びなさい。

① Fat acts like lighter fluid while sugar acts like charcoal in the grill.

② Fat in the body never runs out while sugar runs out quickly.

③ Sugar helps people to be immune from some infectious diseases while fat keeps people fit.

④ Fat starts burning in the body at the first stage while sugar begins to burn later.

語　数：487 語
出題校：関西学院大

Last summer we watched a young boy build a sand castle at the beach. He 🔊1-35 approached his task with the seriousness of a construction engineer working on a forty-story building. He worked so hard gathering sand that after a half hour he had a large heap of it, which he then with great effort patted into a low building. When he was

5 finally satisfied with his work, he went over to his father.

"Look, Dad. Look what I did."

The boy's father carefully studied the heap. He walked around it as if inspecting 🔊1-36 a work of art.

"Charlie, you've made a great castle. I think it's the best on the beach."

10 The boy's smile was as bright as the sun emerging after a week of rain. His father's praise had made him the happiest boy in the world. As we watched this scene, it reminded us of the power of praise. And sadly, of how little most of us receive as adults.

We thought of a story our friend Marty told us. Marty is a management consultant. 🔊1-37

15 He was hired by an Internet company that was just starting its business. People were too busy and (1)<u>their tempers were reaching the boiling point</u>. There were a lot of disputes among them. Toni, a brilliant young woman and a key member of the technical staff, had been working fourteen hours a day, seven days a week. She said to Marty that a number of job offers were coming her way, and she was tempted to take one.

20 Marty took her aside and asked if there was anything he could do to keep her at the company.

"I think you've been doing a great job, but I also have noticed that your stress level is approaching Mt. Everest. What can I do to help?" Before she could answer, Toni broke down into tears. When she pulled herself together, Marty discovered that in

25 addition to the stress of the long hours and the pressure, she hadn't received one word of approval, let alone praise, of her work. Marty immediately went to Toni's boss and told him (2)<u>the situation</u>.

"And while you're at it," he concluded, "a few words of praise for the rest of the staff could only help."

30 The boss acted immediately on Marty's suggestion. An hour after talking to Toni 🔊1-38 alone in his office, he called all the employees into the conference room. There on the table was a display of sweets and coffee. (3)<u>He then proceeded to tell each person how much he appreciated what they had accomplished.</u> From then on he made it a point

to praise an employee when a job was well done.

    "It was a different place after that," Marty told us. "The boss learned (4)<u>a valuable</u> 35 <u>lesson</u> which he's never forgotten. And, by the way, Toni became a vice-president and is still with the company. She's really happy she didn't take another offer."

❶ 下線部（1）の内容に最も近いものを、1つ選びなさい。 （関西学院大）

  ① they were almost at the point of losing their temper

  ② they have been successful in keeping their temper

  ③ they had finally lost their temper

  ④ they were recovering their temper

❷ 下線部（2）の内容を日本語で説明しなさい。 （関西学院大・改）

_____

_____

❸ 下線部（3）を、he が何を指すのかを明確にしながら日本語にしなさい。

_____

_____

❹ 下線部（4）の内容を 30 字以内の日本語で説明しなさい。

❺ 本文の内容と一致するものを2つ選びなさい。 （関西学院大・改）

  ① The boy felt very happy because of his parent's response to his work.

  ② Marty found that workers in the Internet company were complaining about their low pay.

  ③ Toni used to be a management consultant.

  ④ Toni kept calm while talking with Marty.

  ⑤ Hearing Marty's suggestion, the boss started to express his appreciation to the employees for their achievement.

❻ Which of the following best describes the theme of this text? （関西学院大）

  ① Praise makes people feel happy.

  ② Stress goes away with a word of greeting.

  ③ The employer's words and attitude don't change the company.

  ④ Satisfaction with your work leads to happiness in your family life.

6

語　数：369 語
出題校：宮城大

In the early 1980s, (1)the Coca-Cola Company ("Coke") was nervous about its future. Once, it had been the (a)dominant soft drink in the world. But Pepsi had been slowly catching up to Coke. In 1972, 18 percent of soft drink users said they drank only Coke, compared with 4 percent who called themselves exclusive Pepsi drinkers. By the early 1980s, Coke had dropped to 12 percent, and Pepsi had risen to 11 percent, despite the fact that Coke was much more widely available than Pepsi and spending at least $100,000,000 more on advertising per year.

Pepsi began running (2)television commercials around the country going head-to-head★ with Coke in what they called the Pepsi Challenge. Dedicated Coke drinkers were asked to take a sip from two glasses, one marked Q and one marked M. Which did they prefer? Almost always, they would say M, and then M would be revealed as Pepsi. When Coke privately did head-to-head blind taste tests of their own, they found the same thing: when asked to choose between Coke and Pepsi, the majority, 57 percent, preferred Pepsi. This news was (b)devastating to Coca-Cola management.

Coke's scientists went back and changed the secret formula to make it a little lighter and sweeter — more like Pepsi. Immediately Coke's market researchers noticed an improvement. They tested hundreds of thousands of consumers all across North America, and in head-to-head blind taste tests, New Coke beat Pepsi by 6 to 8 percentage points. Coca-Cola executives were (c)elated. The new drink was given the green light★.

However, it was a disaster. Coke drinkers rose up in outrage against New Coke. There were protests around the country. Coke was in a crisis, and just a few months later, the company was forced to bring back the original formula as Classic Coke. The (3)predicted success of New Coke never happened. But there was an even bigger surprise. (4)For the last twenty years, Coke has competed with Pepsi, with a product that taste tests say is inferior, and it is still the number one soft drink in the world. The story of New Coke, in other words, is a really good example of how complicated it is to find out what people really think.

　　★ head-to-head「一対一の」　★ green light「ゴーサイン」

14

1 下線部（1）の原因を 25 字以内の日本語で説明しなさい。

2 下線部（2）の具体的な内容を日本語で説明しなさい。

_____

_____

_____

3 下線部（a）〜（c）の各語とほぼ同じ意味のものを 1 つずつ選びなさい。 （宮城大・改）

(a)　① worst　　　　② newest　　　③ leading　　　④ latest

(b)　① great　　　　② disastrous　　③ encouraging　④ favorable

(c)　① sophisticated　② sad　　　　③ delighted　　④ discouraged

4 下線部（3）の内容に最も近いものを 1 つ選びなさい。

① New Coke would be lighter and sweeter than ever.

② New Coke would be preferred to Pepsi.

③ New Coke would be put on the market.

④ New Coke would contribute to sales of Classic Coke.

5 下線部（4）を日本語にしなさい。 （宮城大）

_____

_____

_____

6 本文のタイトルとして最も適切なものを 1 つ選びなさい。 （宮城大）

① How Coke Lost the Cola War with Pepsi

② Coke and Pepsi: Friends Forever

③ How New Coke Became Number One

④ A Product's Success Is Hard to Predict

⑤ The Importance of Taste Test Results

語　数：415 語
出題校：北里大

For many humans, social distancing feels like the most unnatural thing in the
world, but in other parts of the natural world, it's the norm. When an infected animal
gets too close, other animals have learned to stay away. To see if animals behaved
differently around infected animals in order to protect themselves from getting sick,
5 researchers have been conducting studies over the past couple decades. ◉ 1-52

Joseph Kiesecker, lead scientist at The Nature Conservancy's* conservation lands
team, worked on one of the earlier studies and found that American bullfrog tadpoles*
were excellent at social distancing. "It was clear they were showing behavior that
when given the choice to be near an infected individual, they avoided that infected
10 individual," he said. ◉ 1-53

Kiesecker placed a tadpole infected with a pathogen* around other healthy
tadpoles. The tadpoles could smell the chemicals from the sick tadpole. Detecting it
was infected, the healthy ones stayed away, according to Kiesecker's findings. ◉ 1-54

During part of the study, Kiesecker also tested keeping a healthy tadpole near an
15 infected one. "When we forced them to stay in close proximity and then observed
whether they were infected or not, the probability that they would get infected increased
based on the proximity that they were to the infected individual," Kiesecker said. ◉ 1-55

Tadpoles aren't the only animals to physically distance themselves from sick
members of their own species. Garden ants also practice social-distancing behaviors
20 when an infected ant is introduced to a group of healthy ants. Nathalie Stroeymeyt,
a lecturer at the University of Bristol's School of Biological Sciences, observed when
ants with a fungal disease* were introduced to a colony of healthy ants. ◉ 1-56

After observing the colonies once the infected ants were introduced, Stroeymeyt
found that unexposed ants stayed away from the exposed ants and the healthy ants
25 stayed further away from each other as well. "We believe (1)this is a proactive measure
to decrease the risk of epidemic transmission through the colony, not unlike the form
of proactive social distancing implemented in our societies to decrease the risk of
transmission of Covid-19," Stroeymeyt said. ◉ 1-57

The lessons learned from these animals aren't exclusive to their own species. ◉ 1-58
30 Epidemiologists* use studies like these, Kiesecker said, to have a better understanding
of how diseases spread amongst other species — including humans. (2)This allows
people to "alter and change their behavior" to decrease the chance of infection, he said.

"Behavior is important," Kiesecker said. "Tadpoles can't watch the news and can't ◉ 1-59 read news articles that tell them this. People can."

　　＊ The Nature Conservancy「1951 年に設立された世界的な自然保護団体（非営利団体）のひとつ」
　　　　bullfrog tadpole「ウシガエルのオタマジャクシ」 pathogen「病原体」 fungal disease「真菌性疾患」
　　　　epidemiologist「疫学者」

1 Regarding Paragraphs 3 and 4, explain in Japanese the experiments that Kiesecker did and the results that he obtained from them.

Paragraph 3
　experiment：_____
　result：_____

Paragraph 4
　experiment：_____
　result：_____

2 Translate the underlined sentence (1) into Japanese. Clarify what "this" refers to.

_____
_____

3 Translate the underlined sentence (2) into Japanese. Clarify what "This" refers to.

_____
_____
_____

4 Which is the best answer for each question?

(1) What was the purpose of the research introduced in the text? (北里大)

　① To see if animals show any proactive measures against the biological attack from other species.

　② To see if animals change their behavior to avoid infected members of their species.

　③ To see if animals can find differences between individuals from their chemical signals.

　④ To see if animals control the behavior of other individuals when they are sick.

(2) According to the text, which of the following statements is true? (北里大・改)

　① We, humans, are better at keeping social distance than other animals because we can use a language to communicate with each other.

　② Diseases are spread very quickly among garden ants because healthy ants tend to be attracted to the chemical substance emitted by sick ones.

　③ Our behavior to prevent Covid-19 is somewhat similar to the behavior of ants in colonies with infected ants.

　④ Infectious diseases can easily end the life of garden ants because they make a colony.

語　数：477 語
出題校：三重大

　　If we don't know why we can't sleep, it's in part because we don't really know why 🔊 1-64
we need to sleep in the first place. We know we miss it if we don't have it. And we
know that (1)no matter how much we try to resist it, sleep conquers us in the end. We
know that seven to nine hours after giving in to sleep, most of us are ready to get up
again, and 15 to 17 hours after that we are tired once more. We have known for 50
years that we divide our slumber* between periods of deep-wave sleep and what is
called rapid eye movement (REM) sleep, when (2)(active / as / as / awake / is / the brain
/ we're / when), but our voluntary muscles are paralyzed*. We know that all mammals
and birds sleep. A dolphin sleeps with half its brain awake so it can remain aware of its
underwater environment. When mallard ducks* sleep in a line, the two outermost birds
are able to keep half of their brains alert and one eye open to guard against predators*.
Fish, reptiles, and insects all experience some kind of repose too.

　　All this downtime* comes (3)at a price. An animal must lie still for a great stretch 🔊 1-65
of time, during which it is easy prey for predators. What can possibly be the payback*
for such risk? "If sleep doesn't serve an absolutely vital function," the renowned sleep
researcher Allan Rechtschaffen once said, "it is the greatest mistake evolution ever
made."

　　The predominant theory of sleep is that the brain demands it. This idea derives in 🔊 1-66
part from common sense — whose head doesn't feel clearer after a good night's sleep?
But the trick is to confirm this assumption with real data. (4)How does sleeping help the
brain? The answer may depend on what kind of sleep you are talking about. Recently,
researchers at Harvard led by Robert Stickgold tested undergraduates* on various
aptitude* tests, allowed them to nap, then tested them again. They found that those
who had engaged in REM sleep subsequently performed better in pattern recognition
tasks, such as grammar, while those who slept deeply were better at memorization.
Other researchers have found that the sleeping brain appears to repeat a pattern of
neuron firing that occurred while the subject* was recently awake, as if in sleep the
brain were trying to commit to long-term memory what it had learned that day.

　　Such studies suggest that memory consolidation* may be one function of sleep. 🔊 1-67
Giulio Tononi, a noted sleep researcher at the University of Wisconsin, Madison,
published an interesting twist* on this theory a few years ago: His study showed that
the sleeping brain seems to weed out redundant or unnecessary synapses* or

connections. So (5)the purpose of sleep may be to help us remember what's important, by letting us forget what's not.

* slumber「眠り、まどろみ」 paralyze「麻痺させる、しびれさせる」 mallard duck「マガモ」 predator「捕食動物」 downtime「停止時間」 payback「見返り」 undergraduate「学部学生」 aptitude「適性」 subject「被験者」 consolidation「定着」 twist「予想外の進展」 synapse「シナプス（神経細胞の連接部）」

1 下線部（1）を、it が何を指すかを明らかにして、日本語にしなさい。 　　　　　　（三重大）

_____

_____

2 下線部（2）が「脳は起きているときと同じくらい活発である」という意味になるように、（　）内の語句 を並べ替えなさい。 　　　　　　（三重大）

_____

3 下線部（3）の "at a price" とは具体的にどういうことか、日本語で簡潔に述べなさい。 　　　　　　（三重大）

_____

_____

4 下線部（4）に関して、Robert Stickgold 氏が率いる研究者たちは、睡眠と脳の働きに関するどのような 実験結果を得たか、2 種類の睡眠に分けて日本語で簡潔に述べなさい。 　　　　　　（三重大）

_____

_____

5 下線部（5）を日本語にしなさい。 　　　　　　（三重大）

_____

_____

6 この記事のタイトルとして最も適切なものを 1 つ選びなさい。

① Why living things need sleep

② Pattern Recognition tasks and memorization

③ How sleep helps memory consolidation

④ Difference of deep-wave sleep and REM sleep

語　数：538 語
出題校：愛知教育大

"Truth" is probably the greatest barrier to good communication.　During an ♦ 1-72 argument with a friend or your spouse★, you may have such a powerful conviction that you are right that you don't try to see the other person's point of view.　Instead, you argue and try to force them to agree with you.　(1)This never works.　You've probably
5　noticed that the more you try to persuade the other person to agree with you, the more argumentative he or she becomes.　This is because you're not really listening to their viewpoint.　They believe their feelings are being ignored, and they'll argue louder and longer to try to get you to listen.　You both end up feeling angry and frustrated.

　　You may be completely unaware you're doing this.　A woman's husband recently ♦ 1-73
10　said, "Sarah, you always do exactly what you want without considering my needs.　You put your career and your needs first."　Sarah replied, "No, I don't.　You are my priority, Harold, but sometimes my studies have to take precedence★ if I have a big exam coming up."　Although Sarah might think she's being honest and reasonable, she has made the mistake of suggesting that she's right and he's wrong about this.　The moment
15　she contradicts★ him, (2)she proves that he's right.　In point of fact, she's not trying to understand his point of view, she's only tuned in★ to her needs and her own view of the situation.　That's exactly what he's complaining about!

　　(3)　So what's the alternative?　She could express her feelings with "I feel" ♦ 1-74 statements.　How does she feel?　She feels ticked off★!　So why not just say this instead
20　of being argumentative?　She could also try to understand what he's thinking and feeling.　How does he feel?　He feels shut out and ignored.　She could say, "I feel put down★ and angry, but I know there's some truth in what you say.　Apparently you think I've put my career first and you feel rejected.　Is this the way you feel?　If so, I could understand why you feel hurt and angry."

25　　(4)　I've worked with hundreds of people with troubled relationships, and ♦ 1-75 practically every one of them has made the same mistake of arguing about the "truth."　This strategy never helped anyone resolve a problem.　When you feel upset, you will have a tremendous urge to explain why your ideas and feelings are valid★.　*Don't do it!*　You will have a tremendous urge to defend yourself and argue.　*Don't do it!*　What
30　usually happens when you try to point out the truth to someone?　When you argued and got defensive, did your spouse ever stop arguing and say, "Thank you, thank you for opening my eyes.　I see now where I was so wrong"?　(A)

　　The key to resolving an argument is often to back off★ and try a different approach. ♦ 1-76

The bottom line is that you must never defend the "truth!" (5)<u>Your "truth" is your</u> 35
<u>enemy!</u> When you give up the idea that you have a monopoly* on the truth and you
try to understand the other person's point of view, you will find that people will be
much more willing to listen to you and to understand your own point of view.

★ spouse「配偶者」　take precedence「優先する」　contradict「否定する」　tune in「耳を傾ける」　tick off「叱責する」
put down「批判する」　valid「正当な根拠のある」　back off「一歩引く」　monopoly「独占権」

1 下線部（1）を、This の内容を明らかにして日本語にしなさい。 （愛知教育大）

_____

_____

2 下線部（2）はどういうことか、日本語で説明しなさい。 （愛知教育大）

_____

_____

_____

3 次の空所に入れるのに最も適当なものを1つ選びなさい。

（ i ） **According to paragraph (3), one example of "I feel" statements may be "(　)".**

① I felt that you were angry with me for no reason.

② You feel you are rejected, but I feel it is completely wrong.

③ I felt that you were criticizing me, but I was wrong. I should have understood your
viewpoint.

④ I'm sorry I couldn't see what you meant, but I feel it is irrational to me.

（ ii ） **According to paragraph (4), you must (　)**

① talk about how you feel and why it is sensible enough.

② not defend yourself by explaining your way of thinking.

③ show "the truth" and explain why it is true.

④ be defensive enough so as not to hurt the other.

4 文中の（A）内に入れるのに適当な文を1つ選びなさい。 （愛知教育大）

① That's what happens! ② Don't do it! ③ It depends!

④ Of course not! ⑤ You are welcome!

5 下線部（5）はどういうことか、本文全体の趣旨に沿って日本語で説明しなさい。 （愛知教育大）

_____

_____

10

語　数：567 語
出題校：名古屋市立大

"Organic": in less than a century, the term has become a symbol of quality and tradition.　Nowadays, we are offered a wealth of organic products never imagined by organic pioneers.　In recent years, products have appeared in shopping areas and superstores claiming to be "100% organic," or to contain "no artificial additives*."　From salads to skincare products, shoppers have an incredible range to choose from.

But how much better are those products than non-organic products?　Do they really help protect the environment?　Are they better for your health?　(1)The one thing you can be sure about is that they'll probably cost twice as much!　So how can you know what you're getting and whether it's worth it?

The largest sector of organic products is still food, both as separate products and as ingredients in everything from breakfast cereals to ice-cream.　Supporters claim that these products taste better and are better for you.　Critics say there is no nutritional difference.

In recent years, public demand for these products has increased enormously, driven by scares over the possible health risks of chemical pesticides.　However, the debate continues over whether or not these risks really exist.　(2)Both sides present evidence from scientific studies.　First, consumers are told that pesticides can cause cancer, especially in children.　Then, other equally qualified scientists say the fears are exaggerated.　So, who can you trust?

Despite denials by many scientists and large agribusinesses, (3)there seems reason to be cautious.　Recently, a study that tested 957 non-organic foods found that 203 still had some pesticides, including nearly all of the bread tested.　While the study claimed that the amounts found were safe, other scientists say our understanding of the effects of pesticides on human health is still very limited.

We don't really know the amount of pesticides we can safely consume.　So it is probably a good idea to consume less of them.　But can you afford to?　Not everyone can pay the high prices necessary to buy organic food regularly. While organic eggs, for example, may cost only 50 percent more than the regular kind, an organic chicken can sometimes cost six times the price of a factory-farmed one.

It's easy to forget that without industrial farming methods, we simply wouldn't have so much cheap food.　Are we prepared to give up meat every day and return to having it less frequently like our grandparents did?

2-8　　　Of course, many people say we should.　They provide not only health reasons but ethical and ecological ones, too.　They argue that we have quickly gone from (4)(food, having, having, little, much, to, too, too), and that we have become used to a way of life that is destroying our environment and harming our health.　Their critics, on the other hand, say (5)it's too idealistic to think we can produce the food the world needs organically.

2-9　　　The main problem with organics seems to be that although it opposes big business, it is also becoming big business.　You may feel that the organic Indonesian oils in your shampoo do wonders for your hair.　But shipping shampoo halfway across the world certainly isn't going to help stop the greenhouse effect.　And does the supermarket selling it to you really care about the conditions of the workers who produce it?　Many organic products are unsustainable.　They may be good for us, but are they good for the planet?　Perhaps we should be replacing the word "organic" with "local" and "hand-made."　Or, perhaps, we should just do like some of our grandparents did and grow our own food.

35

40

45

　　　★ additive: a substance that is added to food to improve its taste, appearance etc.

1　下線部（1）を、they の内容を明らかにしながら日本語に訳しなさい。

_____

_____

2　下線部（2）の Both sides が指している語を、第 1 ～ 4 段落の中から英語 1 語でそれぞれ抜き出しなさい。

（名古屋市立大）

_____

_____

3　下線部（3）の reason の具体的内容を、本文に即して日本語で答えなさい。

_____

_____

4　下線部（4）（food, having, having, little, much, to, too, too）を、本文の意味が通るように並べ替えなさい。

（名古屋市立大）

_____

→次頁へ

5 下線部（5）を日本語に訳しなさい。 （名古屋市立大・改）

_____

_____

6 本文の内容と合っているものには○、そうでないものには×をつけなさい。 （名古屋市立大・改）

① The term "organic" has been popular for more than one hundred years.

② Products that are most commonly put on the organic market are shampoos.

③ The high price of organic foods could prevent us from eating such foods every day.

④ Consumers' demands have made the organic industry grow rapidly.

⑤ Indonesian oils can reduce the greenhouse effect.

MEMO

語　数 : 533 語
出題校 : 法政大

The spread of driver-assistance technology will be gradual over the next few years. 　2-14
However, in the not-too-distant future fully (a)autonomous cars will most likely become
a reality. When they do, they will make (b)existing cars look as old-fashioned as steam
engines* and landline telephones*.

For a vision of this future, visit Heathrow airport outside London, and head to　2-15
a "pod* parking" area. Transfers between the car park and terminal are provided
by driverless electric pods moving on dedicated roadways above the street. Using a
touchscreen kiosk, you summon a pod and specify your destination. A pod, which
can seat four people, pulls up, parks itself, and opens its doors. Jump in, sit down, and
press the start button. It drives you to your destination, avoiding other pods and neatly
parking itself when you arrive, before heading off to pick up its next passengers.

(c)Self-driving cars have enormous benefits. Today 94% of car accidents are due　2-16
to human error, and the three leading causes are alcohol, speeding, and interruptions.
Accidents kill around 1.2 million people a year worldwide. (d)Driverless cars cannot
drink alcohol, break the speed limit, or get interrupted by a text message, so accidents
should occur much less often. A new study estimates that (1)if 90% of cars on American
roads were autonomous, the number of accidents would fall from 5.5 million a year to
1.3 million, and road deaths from 32,400 to 11,300.

As well as being safer, self-driving vehicles would make traffic flow more smoothly,　2-17
because they would not brake unpredictably, could be routed to avoid crowded roads,
and could travel close together. All of these factors would increase road capacity. A
study by the University of Texas estimates that (2)if 90% of cars in America were self-
driving it would be equivalent to a doubling of road capacity. Delays would be cut by
60% on motorways and 15% on suburban roads. And riders in self-driving vehicles
would be able to do other things. The resulting productivity gains would be worth $1.3
trillion a year in America and $5.6 trillion worldwide. Children, the elderly and the
disabled could gain more independence.

(3)With cars in constant use, much less parking space would be needed. Parking　2-18
accounts for as much as 24% of the area of American cities. Some urban areas have
as many as 3.5 parking spaces per car; even so, people looking for parking account for
30% of total driving time in urban business districts. By liberating space wasted on
parking, autonomous vehicles could allow more people to live in city centers; but they
would also make it easier for workers to live farther out. If you can sleep on the trip, a

longer commute becomes feasible.

2-19   Car-lovers will doubtless regret the passing of machines that, in the 20th century, 35
became symbols of personal freedom. But in a future without drivers, people will come
to wonder why they tolerated such a high rate of road deaths, and why they spent so
much money on machines that mostly sat unused. A world of self-driving vehicles may
sound odd, but coming generations will probably consider the era of car ownership to
have been much stranger. 40

　* steam engine「蒸気機関車」　landline telephone「固定電話」　pod「ポッド（カプセル状の乗り物）」

1　本文中の下線部（a）〜（d）の中から、意味の異なるものを１つ選びなさい。 　（法政大）

2　下線部（1）のように予測される理由を、簡潔な日本語で説明しなさい。

_____

_____

3　下線部（2）のように予測される理由を、簡潔な日本語で説明しなさい。

_____

_____

4　下線部（3）を日本語にしなさい。

_____

_____

5　本文の内容に関する次の問いの答えとして最も適切なものを、それぞれ１つずつ選びなさい。 　（法政大）

(A)　In addition to increasing road capacity, what effects would self-driving cars have
　　on society?
　　①　lower taxes and carbon dioxide emissions
　　②　make driving more exciting and competitive
　　③　increase economic efficiency and mobility for more people
　　④　reduce the number of police cars and ambulances on roads

(B)　What is the best title for this passage?
　　①　The dangers of self-driving cars
　　②　Long-term research key to vehicle safety
　　③　Self-driving cars to change the world
　　④　Coexistence between new and traditional technologies

Advances in technology over the past 200 years have been remarkable and have ⊙2-24 brought us many benefits. However, the integration of technology into society has not always been smooth. The first industrial revolution began in Britain in the late 18th century. Machines developed at the time could make clothes much more efficiently, easily, and cheaply than before. Even so, not everyone felt happy about (1)this at first. Groups of skilled weavers and textile machine operators, known as Luddites, feared that their jobs would be taken away. They began a labor movement in order to protest and resist the widespread use of the new technology by factory owners. Their protest actions included destroying machines — crimes for which some Luddites were killed by authorities.

As we now know, these technological advances did not slow down. Over time, ⊙2-25 they became widely accepted and appreciated. Before long, other innovations like the steam engine were powering heavy machinery across Europe and beyond. The second industrial revolution, toward the end of the 1800s, brought the gasoline engine and the use of electricity. The third industrial revolution, in the late 20th century, produced computers as well as digital technologies and communications. And, recently, experts have declared that developments in artificial intelligence (AI) and advanced robotics have led us into the fourth industrial revolution.

Even today, however, we hear warnings about (2)the potentially harmful effects of ⊙2-26 contemporary technologies. Some observers claim that the latest AI inventions could have negative impacts on workers, businesses, and society as a whole. The main concern, as in past eras, is that machines will replace humans in the workplace. These observers suggest that a large number of occupations might be lost to AI and robots in the next few years. Taxi and truck drivers, cleaners, and factory workers are among those considered to be at risk.

The fear is even expressed that the AI revolution might lead to mass unemployment. ⊙2-27 According to some experts, up to 800 million jobs could be lost globally by 2030. Moreover, the workers who will lose their jobs to machines are likely to be those with fewer skills and less education, increasing the gap between rich and poor. Some people believe that this will create social conflict and instability.

However, we do not necessarily need to take such a negative outlook on the future. ⊙2-28 While some job losses due to AI-powered technologies will occur, there will not be an overall decrease in employment. New jobs will appear, and humans will always be needed to supervise and maintain the robots. And there are many jobs which machines just cannot do, such as those involving social relationships and interpersonal skills. For instance, a machine would have trouble replacing a friendly salesperson, or a kind and compassionate care giver. Indeed, in a recent report for the Organization for Economic Cooperation and Development, (3)researchers predicted that not as many jobs will disappear as had previously been thought.

So how can we make the smoothest possible transition into the new era that the fourth industrial revolution has brought? It is important to recognize and respond to the impacts of technological inventions on people's lives. Governments must provide retraining and new opportunities for those workers who lose their jobs. Also, when many jobs disappear in specific regions, it will be necessary to bring new high-tech industry to those towns and cities.

People experienced fears of being displaced by machines during previous industrial revolutions. However, the new technologies actually created new employment opportunities and ended up enhancing our lives significantly. Keeping in mind both the conflicts and the successes of the past, let's cooperate today in creating the best shape for our AI-powered future together.

1 下線部 (1) の内容を本文に即して日本語で説明しなさい。

_____

_____

2 第2段落の情報に基づいて、次の①〜④の発明品がどの産業革命で誕生したものか、空所に適切なものをそれぞれ1つずつ入れなさい。　(滋賀県立大・改)

① light bulbs　② self-driving cars　③ steam-powered trains　④ the Internet

第一次産業革命（　　　）　　　第二次産業革命（　　　）

第三次産業革命（　　　）　　　第四次産業革命（　　　）

3 下線部 (2) の具体的内容を、本文に即して20字以内の日本語で説明しなさい。（句読点も含む）

→次頁へ

Which groups of people are considered most likely to lose their jobs to AI?

① both rich and poor people

② business people and global researchers

③ managers and supervisors

④ unskilled and untrained workers

❺ 下線部（3）を日本語にしなさい。 (滋賀県立大)

_____

_____

❻ 本文の内容と一致するものを2つ選びなさい。 (滋賀県立大・改)

① Some people hope humans are replaced by machines.

② Some people see AI as a threat to society.

③ Authorities should ignore areas where many jobs are lost.

④ Governments should provide help for workers and regions that lose jobs.

⑤ People must refuse to recognize and respond to revolutionary changes.

❼ 本文の主旨に最も近いものを1つ選びなさい。 (滋賀県立大)

① AI can be smoothly integrated into society, bringing jobs and other benefits.

② AI will probably not be integrated into society smoothly.

③ Unemployment was a problem in the past, but it will not be in the future.

④ Unemployment will increase due to AI and robotics.

MEMO

An ant rushes over a sandy beach on a path full of twists and turns. It turns right, left, back, then halts, and moves ahead again. How can we explain the complexity of the path it chose? We can think up a sophisticated program in the ant's brain that might explain its complex behavior, but we'll find that it does not work. What we have overlooked in our efforts to speculate about the ant's brain is (1)the ant's environment. The structure of the wind-and-wave-molded beach, its little hills and valleys, and its obstacles shape the ant's path. The apparent complexity of the ant's behavior reflects the complexity of the ant's environment, rather than the ant's mind. The ant may be following a simple rule: get out of the sun and back to the nest as quickly as possible, without wasting energy by climbing obstacles such as sand mountains and sticks. Complex behavior does not imply complex mental strategies.

A lone, hungry rat runs through what psychologists call a T-maze★. It can turn either left or right. If it turns left, it will find food in eight out of ten cases; if it turns right, there will only be food in two out of ten cases. The amount of food it finds is small, so it runs over and over again through the maze. Under a variety of experimental conditions, rats turn left most of the time, as one would expect. But sometimes they turn right, though (2)this is the worse option, puzzling many a researcher. According to the logical principle called (3)*maximizing*, the rat should always turn left, because there it can expect food 80 percent of the time. Sometimes, rats turn left in only about 80 percent of the cases, and right 20 percent of the time. Their behavior is then called *probability matching*, because it reflects the 80/20 percent probabilities. It results, however, in a smaller amount of food; (4)the expectation is only 68 percent. The rat's behavior seems irrational. Has evolution miswired★ the brain of this poor animal? Or are rats simply stupid?

We can understand the rat's behavior once we look into its natural environment rather than into its small brain. Under the natural conditions of foraging★, a rat competes with many other rats and animals for food. If all go to the spot that has the most food, each will get only a small share. The one mutant★ organism that sometimes chooses the second-best patch would face less competition, get more food, and so be favored by natural selection. Thus, rats seem to rely on (5)a strategy that works in a competitive environment but doesn't fit the experimental situation, in which an individual is kept in social isolation.

The stories of the ant and the rat make (6)the same point. In order to understand behavior, one needs to look not only into the brain or mind but also into the structure of the physical and social environment.

* T-maze「T型迷路」　miswire「誤った造りにする」　foraging「エサをあさること」　mutant「突然変異の」

1 下線部（1）の具体的な内容を日本語で説明しなさい。 (弘前大)

_____

_____

2 下線部（2）のように言える理由を、this が指している内容を明らかにして日本語で説明しなさい。 (弘前大)

_____

_____

3 下線部（3）の説明として最も適当なものを 1 つ選びなさい。
① choosing the best cost effective alternative
② aiming to achieve only satisfactory results
③ choosing the alternative with the best or highest expected outcome
④ generating creative ideas through intensive group discussion.

4 下線部（4）の説明になるように、空所に適当な数字を入れなさい。

If there are two possible ways, (a)(　　　)% of the rats turn left to go to a place where there is an (b)(　　　)% probability of finding food. In that case, the probability of finding food is 64%. In the same way, if 20% of the rats turn right to go to a place where there is a (c)(　　　)% probability of finding food, the probability of finding food is (d)(　　　)%. Thus, the expectation is 68%.

5 下線部（5）について、次の（ア）、（イ）の質問にそれぞれ日本語で答えなさい。 (弘前大)
（ア）　ここで説明されている strategy は、具体的にネズミのどのような行動について述べたものか。

_____

_____

（イ）　この strategy は、competitive environment ではうまくいくが、experimental situation には合わないものであるとされている。それはなぜか。

_____

_____

6 下線部（6）の具体的な内容を日本語で説明しなさい。 (弘前大)

_____

_____

14

語　数：412 語
出題校：広島大

Can you blame the scorching weather on climate change? Not really. Or at least not yet. In a National Oceanic and Atmospheric Administration* (NOAA) report released last week, researchers attempted to determine how much they could attribute six extreme weather events last year to human-caused global warming. Even now, months on, some experts worry that drawing conclusions is too sudden. (1)<u>Figuring out what caused a flood in Thailand or a drought in Texas is hard. Doing it quickly is harder.</u>

Scientists involved in NOAA's report thought that climate change did significantly increase the likelihood of last year's warm winter in the United Kingdom and heat wave in Texas, though their calculations are admittedly imperfect. Experts also determined they could not show that global warming contributed to flooding in Thailand — the level of rainfall wasn't historically unusual.

The conclusion? Anyone who, in the midst of a hurricane here or a heat wave there, simplistically blames greenhouse gas emissions is wrong. But it's also wrong to blame all extreme events on forces beyond human control.

Repeated climate patterns such as El Niño and La Niña can influence extreme weather. But natural variability doesn't mean human activity hasn't been playing an increasing role in the formation of (2)<u>extreme events</u>, or in the scale of the resulting damage. Most obviously, more people are living in environmentally insecure zones. (3)<u>Stripping land or degrading wetlands can leave humans more vulnerable to floods</u>, as in Thailand, or hurricanes, as in New Orleans.

And the planet is certainly warming. Humans releasing heat-trapping gases into the atmosphere are almost certainly responsible for much, if not all, of that warming; the particular patterns of warming, comparison to the historical record, and the basic principles of physics all indicate this. On average, more energy in the system probably increases the intensity or frequency of certain extreme weather events, such as very high temperatures, across the planet. Patterns emerge. In recent years, there have been more record-breaking heat events and fewer record-breaking cold ones. Scientists are also beginning — but only beginning — to assess how much particular incidents can be attributed to climate change in anything like real time.

So, while (4)<u>the science of attribution</u> improves, what can you say the next time you're suffering from a sustained heat wave? This is the sort of thing that will get more common across a warming world. (5)<u>That should be more than enough to spur Americans to demand action from their leaders.</u>

* National Oceanic and Atmospheric Administration「アメリカの海洋大気庁」

1 下線部（1）を日本語にしなさい。 (広島大)

_____

_____

2 下線部（2）の具体例を本文から 3 例抜き出しなさい。

・_____

・_____

・_____

3 下線部（3）を日本語にしなさい。 (広島大)

_____

_____

4 下線部（4）の定義として最も適切なものを 1 つ選びなさい。 (広島大・改)

① the science that is concerned with studying the structure of substances

② the scientific approach to identify the causes of some events

③ the scientific study of forces such as heat, light, sound, and so on

④ the scientific study of general weather conditions

⑤ the study of the environment and the way living things live together and affect each other

5 この記事の中で筆者は、地球温暖化問題についてどのようなことを訴えているか。下線部（5）を手がかりに、日本語で簡潔に説明しなさい。 (広島大)

_____

_____

6 本文の内容と一致するものを 2 つ選びなさい。

① Researchers swiftly determined causes of six extreme weather events in the NOAA report.

② Experts failed to show that global warming led to last year's flood in Thailand.

③ It is wrong to blame greenhouse gas emissions for all of the current hurricanes or heat waves.

④ It is no use encouraging Americans to demand action from their leaders.

We are already aware that our every move online is tracked and analyzed. But you couldn't have known how much Facebook can learn about you from (1)the smallest of social interactions — a 'like'*.

2-53

Researchers from the University of Cambridge designed (2)a simple machine-learning system to predict Facebook users' personal information based solely on which pages they had liked.

2-54

"We were completely surprised by the accuracy of the predictions," says Michael Kosinski, lead researcher of the project. Kosinski and colleagues built the system by scanning likes for a sample of 58,000 volunteers, and matching them up with other profile details such as age, gender, and relationship status. They also matched up those likes with the results of personality and intelligence tests the volunteers had taken. The team then used their model to make predictions about other volunteers, based solely on their likes.

2-55

The system can distinguish between the profiles of black and white Facebook users, getting it right 95 percent of the time. It was also 90 percent accurate in separating males and females, Democrats and Republicans. Personality traits like openness and intelligence were also estimated based on likes, and were as accurate in some areas as a standard personality test designed for the task. Mixing what a user likes with many kinds of other data from their real-life activities could improve these predictions even more. Voting records, utility bills and marriage records are already being added to Facebook's database, where they are easier to analyze. Facebook recently partnered with offline data companies, which all collect this kind of information. (3)This move will allow even deeper insights into the behavior of the web users.

2-56

Sarah Downey, a lawyer and analyst with a privacy technology company, foresees insurers using the information gained by Facebook to help them identify risky customers, and perhaps charge them with higher fees. But there are potential benefits for users, too. Kosinski suggests that Facebook could end up as an online locker for your personal information, releasing your profiles at your command to help you with career planning.

2-57

Downey says the research is the first solid example of the kinds of insights that can be made through Facebook. "This study is a great example of how the little things you do online show so much about you," she says. "You might not remember liking things, but Facebook remembers and (4)it all adds up."

2-58

* a 'like'：フェイスブック上で個人の好みを表示する機能。日本語版のフェイスブックでは「いいね！」と表記される。

1 下線部 (1) の意味に最も近いものを 1 つ選びなさい。 (法政大)

① communicating with other people in insignificant ways

② expressing little ambition for social achievement

③ having only a small hope for your success in society

④ making an unimportant deal in your daily life

2 下線部 (2) の構築に利用した情報やデータを 3 つ、日本語で箇条書きにしなさい。

- _____
- _____
- _____

3 Kosinski ら研究者が集めたデータをもとに、ユーザーについて「予想できるものとして文中に挙げられていないもの」を 1 つ選びなさい。 (法政大)

① age　　② gender　　③ personality　　④ race

4 下線部 (3) を、This move の内容を明らかにして日本語にしなさい。

_____

_____

5 下線部 (4) の意味に最も近いものを 1 つ選びなさい。 (法政大)

① Your information disappears before long.

② Your information declines in the long run.

③ Your database vanishes after all.

④ Your data accumulates in the end.

6 本文の内容に一致するものを 1 つ選びなさい。 (法政大)

① Researchers from the University of Cambridge created a model which can predict personal details of Facebook users through their preferences.

② The volunteers disclosed their personal information and matched up their own profile with those of others.

③ Some private companies foresee potential risks for their business due to the cost of the computer learning system.

④ The newly developed computer program will play a significant role in the future in protecting personal information.

語　数：452 語
出題校：岩手大

Have you heard the well-known claim that only 7 percent of any spoken message is 2-63
based on verbal communication? So-called experts tell us that a full 93 percent of any
message is communicated nonverbally. This contention is, of course, absolute rubbish.

The 7-percent formula is endorsed by many professional communication trainers. 2-64
They tell us that of the 93 percent figure referring to nonverbal communication, 55
percent is through body language and the other 38 percent is through tone of voice.

I attended a communications workshop recently in which the facilitator* quite 2-65
confidently emphasized (1)these statistics. I was, to put it indelicately, dumbfounded*.
I challenged her by asking, "Do you mean that if I stood in front of this class and spoke
in Chinese, as long as my body language and tone of voice were consistent with my
message, you would all understand me?" She used all the communication skills at her
command to virtually slap me down. She supported her claims by quoting the research
done by the eminent psychology professor Albert Mehrabian.

(2)The rest of the class, impressed that this principle was being put forth as the 2-66
result of a scientific study and not just as a myth or rumor, nodded in agreement. I
acquiesced*, remaining unconvinced.

I consulted my friend Google and did some research. Yes, experiments were 2-67
conducted by Albert Mehrabian, currently professor emeritus* of psychology at the
University of California at Los Angeles. But (3)the research in question was done in
1967, using one word at a time to measure what the listener believed to be the feeling of
the speaker and determine if the listener liked the speaker. The experiment was never
intended to measure how well the listeners understood what the speaker was trying to
communicate.

Mehrabian has published his work and findings in the book *Silent Messages*. On 2-68
his website, Mehrabian states: "*Silent Messages* contains a detailed discussion of my
findings on inconsistent messages of feelings and attitudes (and the relative importance
of words vs. nonverbal cues)." I found that the professor says (4)his findings have been
misquoted. Max Atkinson, a communications researcher in Wells, Somerset, United
Kingdom, quoted from a personal e-mail he received from Mehrabian; in the e-mail,
Mehrabian said:

"I am obviously uncomfortable about misquotes of my work. From the very 2-69
beginning, I have tried to give people the correct limitations of my findings.
Unfortunately, the field of self-styled 'corporate image consultants' or 'leadership

consultants' has numerous practitioners with very little psychological expertise."

I learned an important lesson from that workshop I attended. (5)I learned not to ₃₅ swallow what some people call "facts" without careful examination of how the so-called facts were obtained, especially the ones that on the surface seem unnatural.

* facilitator「司会者」 dumbfounded「あぜんとした」 acquiesce「黙従する」 professor emeritus「名誉教授」

1 下線部（1）の these statistics の具体的な内容を日本語で説明しなさい。 (岩手大)

_____

_____

2 下線部（2）を日本語にしなさい。 (岩手大)

_____

_____

3 下線部（3）の目的は何だったのかを、本文の内容に即して 70 字以内の日本語で説明しなさい。 (岩手大・改)

_____

4 下線部（4）の内容を最も的確に説明しているものを 1 つ選びなさい。

① People have not appreciated what Mehrabian found.

② People have avoided mentioning Mehrabian's findings.

③ People have been saying Mehrabian's findings are wrong.

④ People have incorrectly repeated what Mehrabian found.

5 下線部（5）を日本語にしなさい。 (岩手大)

_____

_____

6 この英文の内容に最も近いことを示しているものを 1 つ選びなさい。

① Better late than never.

② Wise men make proverbs and fools repeat them.

③ Much learning makes men mad.

④ A man who asks is a fool for five minutes. A man who never asks is a fool for life.

語　数：569 語
出題校：西南学院大

Since the start of the modern planet-hunting era more than 15 years ago, scientists have said their search wasn't about astronomy; it was about biology. These planet hunters are looking for earth-like life on distant worlds. That means the planets would have to be like ours too. They'd have to be about the same size. They'd have to have the same rocky core. (1)They'd also have to travel around their parent stars at just the right distance to have liquid water, the main ingredient for life. Scientists call this the habitable zone.

But while the big discovery hasn't been made yet, researchers might be getting close. At a recent conference in Wyoming, a team of European scientists announced the discovery of at least 50 new worlds. One of them, called (2)Goldilocks, circles a star about 36 light-years away in the constellation Vela★. The planet sits just inside its sun's habitable zone, though it is four times closer to its sun than the Earth is to ours. "It's a beautiful detection," says Geoff Marcy, who leads a different team of planet hunters at the University of California, Berkeley. "And it could possibly be habitable."

(3)Possible is the best anyone can say for now. A clearer answer will have to wait for more powerful telescopes to be built. If the answer turns out to be yes, the question of whether Goldilocks actually is home to life will depend on (4)many factors. To start with, does it have any water? Does it have a solid, rocky surface on which life can live? Does it have a cooling cloud layer to avoid overheating from its sun?

Nobody knows. It would be an unlikely bit of luck if the newly discovered world did have all (5)the right stuff for life. After all, so many conditions must be present. The newly discovered world is still a big deal, though. It proves that astronomers now have the technology to find these kinds of planets.

Most of the big planet announcements over the past two years have come from the Kepler space mission. The Kepler mission uses a high-powered orbiting telescope to search a section of the Milky Way galaxy★ for earth-like planets. In particular, it is used to study regular decreases in the brightness of stars. These tiny decreases in brightness are created by planets passing in front of their stars as they orbit.

The 50 new planets announced in Wyoming were discovered from the ground with a device called the High Accuracy Radial velocity Planet Searcher, or HARPS. HARPS uses a telescope at the European Southern Observatory in Chile to look for a star's slight (6)wobble. A wobble is a small change in a star's position as a planet travels around it. Wobbles occur when the gravity of an orbiting planet pulls the star one way, then the other. The very first "exoplanets" — planets that orbit distant stars other than our sun — were found this way.

2-81   With so many unanswered questions, it's still a long shot that Goldilocks will turn out to be the first known exoplanet to support life. Even so, its discovery shows how far planet hunting has come. (7)<u>With all of the searches going on worldwide, and with increasingly powerful technologies, it's just the beginning in what could be a series of extraordinary discoveries that add further evidence to support the notion that humans are not alone in the universe.</u>

40

　　* constellation Vela「帆座（ほざ）」　the Milky Way galaxy「銀河系宇宙」

1　下線部 (1) を They の内容を明らかにして日本語にしなさい。

_____

_____

2　下線部 (2) の特徴を日本語で説明しなさい。

_____

_____

_____

3　下線部 (3) の内容に近いものを 1 つ選びなさい。　　　　　　　　　　　　（西南学院大）

①　It is really great that scientists can see some possibility at present.

②　For the time being, scientists can only say it might be possible.

③　It may be possible for everyone to say it's the best for the time being.

④　At present, people are limited to talking about what is possibly the best.

4　下線部 (4) の具体的な内容を 3 つ、簡潔な日本語で答えなさい。

・_____

・_____

・_____

5　下線部 (5) の意味に最も近いものを 1 つ選びなさい。　　　　　　　　　　（西南学院大）

①　undamaged things　　　　②　correct answers

③　necessary elements　　　　④　extra things

6　下線部 (6) の現象について、それがどのようにして発生するのかも含めて日本語で説明しなさい。

_____

_____

7 下線部 (7) を日本語にしなさい。

_____

_____

_____

8 本文の内容に一致するものを 2 つ選びなさい。 （西南学院大・改）

① To get clear answers about actual conditions on Goldilocks, scientists will need improved technology.

② It appears that Goldilocks has water, a rocky surface, and clouds surrounding it.

③ Fifty new planets were discovered at a recent conference in Wyoming.

④ Though many questions remain, the finding of Goldilocks demonstrates the advances science has made in the search for other planets.

MEMO

語　数：720 語
出題校：北海道大

Think about all your important beliefs and ideas. They may relate to what you study, how you view yourself and others, your political viewpoints, and religious beliefs. Now ask yourself if you prefer to look for evidence that supports and strengthens those ideas, or do you like to look for evidence that might weaken or disprove them? According to social psychologists, we often look for ways to confirm our views, and often avoid attacking them.

Peter Wason first explored this almost sixty years ago in a classic experiment. He presented twenty-nine psychology undergraduates with three numbers: 2, 4, and 6. They were told that their goal was to figure out a particular rule that explained this series of numbers. The actual rule used was very simple: the second number had to be larger than the first number, and the third number had to be larger than the second one. To help them complete the task, the students were allowed to write down any series of three numbers and show them to the experimenter. Every time the numbers matched the rule, the experimenter would tell them it was a match, but wouldn't explain the reason. They could (1)do this as many times as they liked until they were sure that they had figured out the rule. At that point, they could write it down and show it to the experimenter. The students were told to continue testing series of numbers and writing down possible rules until they arrived at the correct one.

Despite the fact that the actual rule was very simple, only six out of the twenty-nine students correctly figured it out on their first attempt. The reason for this was that the students spent most of their time trying to positively test their first ideas. For example, some of the students started by guessing that the rule related to the use of even numbers. They would then *only* write examples that included even numbers until they had persuaded themselves that the rule could only be about those numbers. What they often didn't do, for example, was include odd numbers in order to (2)negatively test their first idea.

This way of thinking is known as *confirmation bias* and it tells us something very important about how we develop our views about the world. When we think about our beliefs, we all feel that the truth is the most important thing for us. However, we are also very powerfully influenced by the way our minds work, and we are often not aware of it. This does not just relate to our preferences for confirming our beliefs rather than disproving them. Social psychologists have also found other influences. For example, we often prefer to continue to believe something because it is useful or emotionally important to us in some way.

2-90   Universities try to address these tendencies by emphasizing the importance of skills   35
like critical thinking and debating. (A), what can often happen is that we only
critically examine new ideas or beliefs we disagree with. (3)There is also some evidence
that debating can actually strengthen your original ideas and beliefs, rather than making
you question them.

2-91   So what can we do to avoid the effects of confirmation bias? One solution is to   40
push ourselves to improve our understanding of different viewpoints. One advantage
of the university seminar system is that (4)students are free to attend the classes of many
different professors. Try to find a professor that disagrees with the ideas that you have
already been taught. In addition, try to carefully read books that you disagree with, and
spend time talking to people that have different ideas from your own. And don't just   45
talk to them, but train yourself to see the conversation through their eyes. You might
feel that they are obviously wrong, but it is important to understand why they feel the
same way towards your ideas. In addition, try to view changing your ideas as exciting
and challenging, and not something uncomfortable, threatening, and negative. It is
very difficult to avoid confirmation bias when you are on your own. It is almost   50
impossible when you are with a group that all agrees with the same idea. The best
place to shape your thinking is therefore somewhere in the messy, ever-changing space
between opposing arguments.

1 下線部 （1） が表す内容を日本語で述べなさい。   (北海道大)

_____

_____

2 第 3 段落で述べられている例において、下線部 （2） に合致する 3 つの数字は以下の①〜④のうちどれか。
2 つ選びなさい。   (北海道大)

① 2，3，4   ② 4，3，2   ③ 2，4，6   ④ 6，4，2

3 空欄 （ A ） に入る最も適切な語句を①〜⑤から 1 つ選びなさい。   (北海道大・改)

① Accordingly   ② For example   ③ However   ④ Similarly   ⑤ Therefore

→次頁へ

4 下線部（3）を日本語に訳しなさい。

---

5 下線部（4）に関連して、次の英文の空所に当てはめるのに最も適切なものを①～④から１つ選びなさい。

（北海道大・改）

The article implies that attending classes of many professors with different views helps you avoid the effects of confirmation bias because (　　　　　).

① books and conversations give you knowledge

② seminars are exciting and challenging

③ you need to justify your ideas

④ you see and compare different ideas

6 本文の内容と一致するものを１つ選びなさい。

① Regardless of their political viewpoints and religious beliefs, we tend to avoid attacking the views of others.

② It rarely happens that we are influenced by our emotions, such as favoring information that confirms our beliefs.

③ Skills of thinking critically and debating are best acquired when we carefully read the books that we disagree with.

④ Placing yourself in a group with different ideas is one of the best ways to avoid confirmation bias.

MEMO

MEMO

Chapter 1

テーマ解説

　ノーベル平和賞を受賞したケニアの活動家、故**ワンガリ・マータイ（Wangari Maathai）**氏が「すでに世界的な資源の争奪戦が始まっている」との警鐘を鳴らして久しい。**鉄鋼(iron and steel)**や**石油(gas)**、精密機械に使われている**レアメタル（rare metal）**などの資源は、爆発的な発展を遂げているインド・中国といった途上国でも需要が高まり、先進国との熾烈な争奪戦を繰り広げている。しかしながら、これらの資源がなくなっても、人々が直接生命の危機にさらされるわけではない。何といっても最も大切な資源は、きれいで**飲用可能な水（drinkable water）**である。このことは、トイレを流す水にすら飲用可能な水をつかっている私たち日本人にとってはピンとこない話かもしれない。しかし、現実にアフリカの女子のなかには、毎日徒歩で何キロも離れたところまで、十分清潔とは限らない水を汲みに行き、しかもそれを何往復もする人も少なくないという。

　アフリカ諸国の内紛や疫病、イスラエル・パレスチナ紛争など、世界的に深刻な問題の多くは少なからず飲用水やそれを巡る争いに原因の一端がある。彼らは、敵が持つ井戸を破壊したり、汚染物質を投入したりする。それが直接相手を殺害するに等しい行為であることを理解しているのである。

▶ 本文出典

　アメリカのサイト Global Health Frontline News の 2010 年 11 月の記事 "Guinea worm's last stand" を基に書かれたものと考えられる。(http://www.ghfn.org/1-topics-general-pages/guinea-worm)

▶ The Carter Center

　1982 年に、カーター元大統領夫妻が設立した非政府組織。紛争の解決や民主化の促進、教育の機会促進、農家へ技術指導など多岐にわたる活動を、世界 80 カ国以上で展開している。

▶ Jimmy Carter

　ジミー・カーター（1924-）。第 39 代アメリカ合衆国大統領。1981 年の大統領退任後は、紛争の解決や貧困の撲滅などへの積極的な活動を続けている。こうした活動が認められ、2002 年にはノーベル平和賞を受賞した。

カーター元大統領とロザリン婦人

▶ Guinea worm disease

　ギニア虫（感染）症。「メジナ虫症」とも呼ばれる。その歴史は古く、『旧約聖書』中の記述「the fiery serpent（火の蛇）」はこの病気のことを指していると考えられている。

　人間の体内で全長 60 cm 以上にまで成長するギニア虫のメスは、幼虫の生育に不可欠な水を求めて、人間の体で水に触れる可能性が高い足付近の皮膚直下まで移動する。感染した人が沼や川に入ると、ギニア虫は、患部から幼虫を数千匹単位で水中に放出する。幼虫はミジンコに摂取され、それが混ざった水を人間が飲んで感染する。

　ギニア虫が人体内を移動するときにかゆみや痛みが発生し、患部が細菌によって二次感染すると、生活が困難なほどの激しい痛みに襲われる。

Chapter 2

▶ 本文出典

　本英文は *Chicken Soup for the Parent's Soul: 101 Stories of Loving, Learning and Parenting* (Mark Victor Hansen, Raymond Aaron, Kimberly Kirberger, & Jack Canfield, Scholastic, 2001) (『親と子を変えた愛の不思議の物語——こころのチキンスープ』ダイヤモンド社　2002 年) の 1 編である "Cyber Step-mother"。「こころのチキンスープ」シリーズの 1 冊目は Mark Victor Hansen と Jack Canfield によって 1993 年に出版された。読者の投稿からなるこの本は口コミで広がり、あっという間にベストセラーとなった。シリーズは 100 冊超、54 カ国以上に翻訳され、売上部数は全世界で 1 億冊を超えている。500 語前後のまとまった英文と心温まる内容から、入試頻出の出典となっている。

Chapter 3

テーマ解説

　チンパンジーやオランウータンなどの類人猿と違い、ヒトがこれほどまでに進化したのは、直立二足歩行が理由であると考えられている。両手が自由になったために、道具を作ったり、火を使ったりすることができるようになった。頭部が安定することによって脳の容量が増え、また、口腔内の筋肉の発達によって高度な言語が使えるようになった—これがヒトの**進化 (evolution)** に関する**仮説 (hypothesis)**の一般的なものである。

　ヒトはアフリカの類人猿の中から進化して誕生したものという仮説、いわゆるサバンナ説がある。アフリカ大陸の気候変動によって食用植物がなくなり、住む場所を変えたり、**狩猟 (hunting)** による肉食に向かった。狩猟のために知恵を絞り、道具を作り、食べやすくするために火を使う—これらの説はヒトの進化を説明するにはもっともらしいものであるが、仮説の域を超えてはいない。もっとも、現人類に共通する女系祖先の一人がアフリカにいたということは、ミトコンドリア DNA の研究によって、ほぼ確実視されているということである。

　チャールズ・ダーウィン (Charles Darwin) が著した『**種の起源**』(***The Origin of Species***) は、生物は**自然選択 (natural selection)** によって、環境に**適応 (adaptation)** するように変化すると説明する。シンプルで理解しやすいこの考え方は、適応進化の要因として、現在でも科学的に認められている。

▶ 本文出典
　イギリスの新聞 *The Guardian* 2011 年 7 月 27 日付の記事から取られたもの。文章全体が調整されている。

▶ Oxford University Museum of Natural History
　オックスフォード大学自然史博物館。1860 年に設立。各種化石や、恐竜、外来昆虫の標本が充実している。ビクトリア朝様式のネオゴシック建築が特徴的である。

Christophe.Finot

オックスフォード大学自然史博物館

▶ Ellie Pearce
　Eiluned Pearce。Robin Dunbar 教授に師事する、博士課程の大学院生。

▶ Robin Dunbar
　Robin Ian MacDonald Dunbar。1947-。英国の人類学者で、進化心理学者。現在は、オックスフォード大学の実験心理学部社会進化神経科学調査グループの団長を勤める。

　一般的には、1990 年代に Dunbar's Number「ダンバー定数」を提唱したことで有名である。この定数は、a theoretical limit to the number of people with whom any individual is able to sustain a stable or meaningful social relationship (usually considered to be roughly 150)「一人一人が安定的で意味のある社会的関係を維持できる、（共同体などの集団における）人々の数の理論的限界（通常、およそ150 と考えられる）」と定義されている。逆に言うと、150 人を超える集団においては、一人一人の性格や習慣的な行動などを互いに理解することができない、ということである。

©2013 Aberdeen University Science Magazine

スコットランドのアバディーン大学で「ネットワークとその普及」と題した講演を行う、ロビン・ダンバー教授（2012 年）

▶ *Biology Letters*
　2005 年より発行されているイギリスの科学誌で、論文審査のある学術専門誌。生物学では有数の権威ある雑誌とされている。

Chapter 4

テーマ解説

　食物の**三大栄養素（three major nutrients）**は**脂肪（fat）**、**タンパク質（protein）**、**炭水化物 / 糖分（carbohydrate / sugar）**である。脳の活動には糖分が不可欠なので、体はさまざまな手段によって糖分を作り出そうとする。まず、血中の糖分がなくなると、肝臓に蓄えられたグリコーゲンを分解して糖分に変える。その分もなくなると、次は筋肉のタンパク質を分解して糖分に変える。無理な**食事制限（diet）**によって筋肉を失った体は、ますます痩せづらくなるというわけである。

　太っていること（fatness）が裕福さの象徴であるのは過去の話らしい。**肥満（obesity）**は、近年の日米英などの先進国で、むしろ低所得者層に多いことが問題になっている。健康的な食品を選んで食べる余裕がないということと、そもそも食生活によって健康で豊かな人生を送ろうという意識が高所得者層よりも希薄なのだという。**貧すれば鈍する（Poverty dulls the wit.）**ということだろうか。

　ファーストフード（fastfood）のように手軽で廉価な食品は、カロリーや脂質が高く、太りやすい。また、味付けが濃いので常習的にもなりやすい。**あなたは食べたものそのものである / 食べるものであなたがどういう人かがわかる（You are what you eat.）**ことを自覚し、食生活には細心の注意を払うべきだろう。

▶ **本文出典**

　Covert Bailey, "Fat: The Primary Fuel," *Smart Exercise: Burning Fat, Getting Fit,* Mariner Books, 1996

▶ **muscle burns both fat and sugar**

fat（脂肪）：動植物に含まれる栄養素の１つ。主に動物の体内に含まれている動物性脂肪は、飽和脂肪酸を多く含んでいるため融点が高い。脂肪はエネルギーとして代謝された場合、炭水化物やタンパク質よりも単位重量あたりの熱量が大きい。したがって哺乳類をはじめとする動物にとって、エネルギー源としての重要度は非常に高い。
sugar（糖）：単糖であるグルコースは細胞の主なエネルギー源である。人間にとっては、思考の際の脳のエネルギー源として非常に重要である。グルコースはグリコーゲンとして体内に蓄えられる。

▶ **antibody**

　「抗体」。体が体内に侵入した異物に反応してできる物質のこと。糖タンパク分子で、特定のタンパク質などの異物（抗原）を認識して、それと結合する働きがあり、主に血液中や体液中に存在する。
　体内に侵入してきた細菌やウイルスなどの抗原と結合することでその抗原の毒素を中和したり、その抗原と抗体の複合体を白血球などに認識させ、殺滅させたり体内から除去させるといった免疫反応を引き起こす働きがある。

Chapter 5

テーマ解説

　社会的な上下関係は、日本においては重要な文化的背景である。例えば、兄弟のうちどちらが年上かということは、家督を決定する重要な要素であり、家族内外の関心事である。また、学校や会社において、年齢的、立場的に目下の者が、然るべき言葉や態度をもって、目上の者に敬意を表すのも自然なことである。一方米国では、とくに必要がなければ brother という表現で済ませてしまうことがほとんどだし、大学において学生が教授をファーストネームで呼ぶのもふつうのことである。これらの違いの説明を**個人主義（individualism）**だけに求めるのは浅薄すぎるかもしれないが、少なくとも個を対等な立場で尊重しようとする傾向は、日本よりも米国の方が強い。

　日本人にとって「褒める」という行為は、基本的に目上の者から目下の者に対するものである。一方米国では、他者に対する評価は社会の相対的な立場に依存することが少ない。「いいものはいい、悪いものは悪い」という、単純ながらも絶対的な評価は、さまざまな人種が集まる米国の社会にとって、最適化された考え方と言えるかもしれない。

▶ **本文出典**

　Howard Kaminsky and Alexandra Penney, "Praise is a short word that goes a long way," *Magic Words: 101 ways to talk your way through life's challenges*, Broadway Books, 2002. から抜粋されたもの。一部調整してある。

Chapter 6

テーマ解説

　ビジネス、とくに**小売業界（retail industry）**においては、**消費者心理（consumer psychology）**と**消費者行動（consumer behavior）**の研究が不可欠である。一般的によく例示される「コンビニ」について極めて簡単に言及すれば、その出店に際して近隣住民の年齢別構成比を吟味して立地場所や店舗方針、取り扱い商品を決めることはもとより、商品の効果的な陳列、さらには天候情報の蓄積までも利用して、消費者心理・行動を分析しているといわれる。

　心理学（psychology）は非常に興味深い実践的な学問である。学問領域は極めて広範にわたって細分化されているが、それを実践・応用する場合には複数の領域が関わってくることも多い。したがって、心理とそれに基づく行動を扱う英文は、ビジネス・教育・脳（認知）・動物・社会・軍事・スポーツなど、さまざまなテーマにおいて見受けられることになる。**反射（reflex）**や**自律（autonomy）**などを除いて、ほとんどすべての行動は「思考・心理」に関わってくるものであるから、それももっともなことだ。

▶ 本文出典

　Malcolm Gladwell, *Blink — The Power of Thinking Without Thinking*, Little, Brown and Company, 2005 の第 3 章 Kenna's Dilemma: The Right — and Wrong — way to Ask People What They Want の一部を抜粋、改変したもの。

▶ Coca-Cola Company ("Coke")

　コカ・コーラ社（コーク）。

　1886 年、アメリカの薬剤師ジョン・S・ペンバートン博士が開発し、友人のフランク・M・ロビンソンが「コカ・コーラ」と名付け、1 杯 5 セントで販売されたのが始まり。同年の売上は一日当たり 9 杯だったが、今では世界中で一日に約 19 億杯ものコカ・コーラ社製品が消費されている。

　"Coke"（コーク）はコカ・コーラの別称。1898 年に Pepsi が名称を Pepsi-cola「ペプシコーラ」にしたため、「コーラ」という名称を「（コカ・コーラに似た）飲料のジャンル名」と捉える人が多くなった。コカ・コーラ社はそれを嫌って、1941 年から広告で「コーク」の名称を使いはじめた。米国では「コカ・コーラ」は「コーラ」ではなく「コーク」と呼ぶことが一般的。

▶ Pepsi

　1894 年、アメリカの薬剤師キャレブ・ブラッドハムが調合した消化不良の治療薬がルーツ。消化酵素のペプシンが名前の由来。

▶ Pepsi Challenge

　1975 年以降、ペプシはコカ・コーラを対象とする比較広告を現在に至るまで断続的に続けている。2014 年時点でも「ペプシ NEX ZERO」と「コカ・コーラ ZERO」の比較調査結果を自社の HP 上に掲載している。

▶ New Coke

　ニュー・コーク。これまでの伝統的な味を変更して 1985 年 4 月に発売された。当初は旧来の商品を併売しなかったが、消費者からの抗議が殺到し、約 3 か月後には併売することになった。「ニュー・コーク」は 1992 年まで規模を縮小しながら販売され、1993 年以降は「Coke II」の名称で変更された。

▶ Classic Coke

　正式名称は Coca cola Classic「コカ・コーラ・クラシック」。1985 年に発売された。2010 年頃から Classic の表記を無くして「コカ・コーラ」に戻している。

Chapter 7

テーマ解説

感染症（**infection**）は、人類にとって文明の誕生以来最大の脅威の１つであり続けている。シルクロード交易によって東アジアから伝播した**ペスト（plague）**が 14 世紀に大流行したことで、欧州の人口の 1/3 が失われたと言われている。中南米のアステカとインカ帝国が滅亡した要因はスペインによる征服だが、実際の最大要因は、西洋人が持ち込んだ**天然痘（smallpox）**の流行による壊滅的な人口の減少だった。**世界保健機関（WHO: The World Health Organization）**の推計によれば、現在も全世界で毎年約 1 千万人が感染症によって死亡している。

感染症は、**ウイルス（virus）**や**細菌（bacteria）**などの**微生物（microorganism）**が体内に侵入し、**繁殖（reproduction）**することで起こる病気である。その最大の特徴は生物間を伝播することで、全ての感染症のうち約半数は人獣共通感染症、つまり人間と**脊椎動物（vertebrate）**の間で伝播可能ということだ。世界保健機関によれば、狂犬病ウイルスを保有するイヌやネコなどに咬まれるなどしてできた傷からのウイルスの侵入が原因で、全世界で毎年 5 万人が死亡している。

予防（prevention）が感染症対策に有効なことは言うまでもないが、驚くべきことに、感染症予防としての「手洗い」にはわずか 160 年ほどの歴史しかない。1847 年にハンガリーの医師イグナーツ・ゼメルヴァイスが「手の消毒をすれば、病気の発症を激減させることができる」ことを証明したが、当初は受け入れられなかった。当時の医学会は、「全ての病気は体のバランスの崩れによるもの」だと考えていたからだ。その後医学は驚くほど発達したが、現在でもウイルスや細菌、さらには感染拡大のメカニズムについて完全に理解できているわけではない。それは、**新型コロナウイルス（COVID-19）**の流行初期に、「感染予防にマスクは有効か」という問いに対する世界保健機関の見解が二転三転したことが裏付けている。つまり、日々**更新（updating）**される**知見（knowledge）**に合わせて、考え方や行動も更新し続ける必要があるのだ。

▶ **本文出典**

本英文は米国ジョージア州に本社を置くニュース専門テレビ局 CNN（Cable News Network）の 2020 年 7 月 27 日の記事から採られている。

記事のタイトルは以下の通り。

> Think social distancing is hard? For these animals, it's second nature
> 「社会的（対人）距離の確保は難しいだろうか？ これらの動物にとっては第 2 の天性である」

▶ **social distancing**

社会的距離。感染拡大を防ぐために物理的な距離をとること。この言葉は 2006 年、効果的な薬もワクチンも存在しない感染症のパンデミックに関する論文において、感染防止対策の１つとして初めて使われた。2020 年に新型コロナウイルス感染症が世界中で蔓延した際に、海外メディアで使われることによって広まった。

一方で social distance という言葉は、1940 年代以降に子どもの社会性に関する研究などにおいて「人間の心理的な距離」を示す言葉として用いられた。その後、黒人や HIV 感染者への偏見から彼らと心理的・社会的に接触を避ける現象を示す言葉として使われるようになった。2020 年以降の日本では、新型コロナウイルス感染症の感染防止のための「物理的な距離」として使用されている。

2020 年 4 月、世界保健機関（WHO）では、それらの意味を明確にするため、感染予防のための物質的な距離を確保することを physical distancing という言葉を用いて表現している。

▶ **The Nature Conservancy**

ザ・ネイチャー・コンサーヴァンシー。TNC と略式表記されることもある。アメリカ合衆国バージニア州の地球環境団体。1951 年設立。非営利団体で、活動内容は生物生息地の確保や稀少野生生物・生態系の保全など。100 万人以上の会員が所属している。1990 年からアジア太平洋地域での活動を開始し、日本には 1999 年に事務所を設立した。

Chapter 8

テーマ解説

　睡眠は、私たちの生活の約3分の1を占める重要なものであるにもかかわらず、いまだ解明されていない部分が多い研究対象である。睡眠は何時間とればよいのか、睡眠時間を多く要する人とそうでない人がいるのはなぜか、睡眠中に私たちの体や脳では何が起きているのか ── などは、誰でも一度は頭をよぎらせたことのある疑問だろう。

　睡眠の話題は、「脳」に関する話題と並んで、自然科学ジャンルの定番として毎年数多くの入試長文で取り上げられている。

　典型的な文脈として、最初に**調査（survey）や実験（experiment）**の内容を紹介し、次にその**結果（consequence / result）**の説明をし、最後にその結果に関する**分析（analysis）**をする、という3段階で構成されているものが多い。

　テーマは、「睡眠不足による心身への影響」「昼寝の効用」といった健康面からのアプローチ、「夢の分析」など夢に関する話題、さらに医学的な見地からの「睡眠と年齢の関係性」「現代人と不眠」など、多岐にわたる。

▶ 本文出典

　アメリカの月刊写真誌 *National Geographic* の 2010 年 3 月号に掲載された、科学作家 D. T. Max の記事を抜粋したもの。原典の見出しは次の通り。

> The Secret of Sleep
> From birth, we spend a third of our lives asleep. After decades of research, we're still not sure why.
> 「睡眠の秘密　生まれてから、我々は人生の3分の1を寝て過ごす。数十年の研究の後も、その理由はまだはっきりとはわからない」

▶ rapid eye movement (REM) sleep

　「レム（睡眠急速眼球運動）睡眠」。体は弛緩して動かないが、目は激しく動き、脳が活動している状態。REM はRapid Eye Movement（急速眼球運動）の頭文字からとられている。レム睡眠の存在は、シカゴ大学のナサニエル・クライトマンとユージン・アゼリンスキーの研究によって、1953 年に明らかになった。

　レム睡眠中に何かの拍子で目が覚めたとき、脳は活動していたため意識はすぐに戻るが、体は弛緩しているためすぐには動かない。この状態が「金縛り」である。

▶ deep-wave sleep

　一般的には non REM sleep「ノンレム睡眠、徐波（じょは）睡眠」と呼ばれ、大脳（cerebrum）は活動を停止しているが、体は起きている状態。「徐波」とは、この状態で発生する脳波の中でも最もゆっくりとした大きな波のことで、「デルタ波」（delta wave）ともいう。

　寝返りをうつのは、体が起きているこの状態の時である。休んでいるのは大脳だけで、脳幹（brain stem：脳の中心部分）はこの状態のときにも起きている。

▶ neuron firing

　ニューロン発火。ニューロン（神経細胞）の電位が自発的かつ急激に上昇する現象のこと。

　人間の脳には 100 億個以上のニューロンがあり、すべての脳の働きは神経細胞間の情報伝達によって行われている。その情報伝達の概要は以下の通り。

　神経細胞が他の神経細胞から刺激（化学物質）を受けると、細胞内の電位が上昇し、ある一定の電位を超えると、自発的に電位が急上昇（ニューロン発火）する。電位上昇によって発生した電気パルスが神経細胞間にある接合部（シナプス）に向けて化学物質を放出させる。そして接合部はその刺激を受けて化学物質を放出し、別の神経細胞を刺激する。（この繰り返しで情報が伝わっていく）

　人間の脳が働いているときは、数十万から数百万の神経細胞が同期して上記の活動をしていると言われている。

▶ Allan Rechtschaffen

　アラン・レヒトシャッフェン。シカゴ大学名誉教授。睡眠の働きや、は虫類、ネズミの睡眠の研究を行う。1968 年にアンソニー・ケイルズと共同で、人間の睡眠の深さを 5 つの「睡眠段階」に分類する国際基準を定義した。

▶ Robert Stickgold

　ロバート・スティックゴールド。ハーバード大学の精神分析学准教授。睡眠と学習の関連を研究し、睡眠不足の危険を指摘している。

Foto: MATTEO RENSI

▶ Giulio Tononi

　ジュリオ・トノーニ。1985 年、イタリアのピサ大学において、睡眠の調節に関する研究で神経科学の学位を取得。2008 年現在、アメリカのウィスコンシン大学マディソン校の精神医学科教授。研究の対象は意識と睡眠。

ジュリオ・トノーニ教授

Chapter 9

テーマ解説

　人間のコミュニケーションは、言葉だけではなく、身振りや顔の表情、声のトーンなど、受け手が五感で感じ取ることができる動作や音などにも大きく依存している。これらの手段を使って情報や意思、感情を伝え、それが円滑に進めば、**共感（sympathy）**が発生し、やがて**信頼関係（relations of trust）**へとつながる。また、双方の持つ背景もコミュニケーションの重要な要素である。言葉が通じず、文化や価値観を共有していない状況では、互いの意図を理解することが容易ではなくなり、誤解が生じる可能性も大きくなる。逆に言えば、相手の文化や価値観を知ることで、コミュニケーションははるかに図りやすくなる。

　コミュニケーション能力（communication skill）の向上は人々にとって大きな関心事である。洋の東西を問わず、その技術を紹介する書籍が数多く出版されていて、その点数は年々増え続けている。そこで紹介されているさまざまな技術の根底にあるのは、相手への関心と**敬意（respect）**を誤解を与えず正確に、そして効果的に伝えるということにほかならない。

Chapter 10

テーマ解説

　オーガニック（organic）という言葉は、一般的に「**化学肥料（chemical fertilizer）**や**化学農薬（chemical pesticide）**などを一切使わずに作られた農産物や、**無添加の（additive-free）**食料品」を指すことが多い。近年は食品だけでなく、化粧品や洗剤、衣料品など、様々な分野で数多くのオーガニック製品が流通している。

　オーガニック食品の根幹をなす**有機農業（organic farming）**は化学農薬や化学肥料を使用しないため、食品への**残留農薬（pesticide residue）**の心配が無い上に、**土壌（soil）**や生態系にとっても影響が少ないとされている。しかし、裏を返せば、雑草の処理や虫の駆除、土壌づくりに人と時間を要するため、オーガニック食品は非オーガニック食品と比べて割高であることが多い。

　環境保護の観点から言えば、オーガニック製品は上述の通り地球環境にとって良いとされることが多い。一方で、オーガニック食品の中心市場が欧米であるのに対し、有機農法を行っている農場のほとんどがアジアや南米にあるため、長距離輸送による**二酸化炭素の排出（carbon dioxide emission）**が地球温暖化につながるのではないか、との懸念もある。

▶ **本文出典**

　Caroline Shackleton and Nathan Paul Turner, *Money Tree: The Business of Organics*, Cambridge University Press, 2014 を一部改変したもの。

▶ **chemical pesticide**

　化学農薬。化学的に合成して作られた農薬のこと。1930年代より欧米で開発が始まり、日本では第二次世界大戦後から広く使われるようになった。1962年にレイチェル・カーソンが著書『*Silent Spring*』（邦訳：沈黙の春）でその危険性を訴えたことが有名。

▶ **industrial farming**

　工業化された農業。工業型農業とも。農作物や畜産物を機械的な手法で、工場のように大量生産すること。農薬や肥料の使用はもちろんのこと、遺伝子組み換え技術も導入し、生産性の最大化を目指す方法。

Chapter 11

テーマ解説

　過去に経験したことがない人口の減少期を迎えつつある日本では、社会を維持するための労働者確保が急務である。人口の減少幅を緩やかにするため、現在政府は少子高齢化対策として、女性や高齢者の就業を促がし、出生率を上げるための政策を実施しているが、国立社会保障・人口問題研究所によれば、2070 年の人口は 8,000 万人を割り込み、2100 年には明治時代末期と同じ約 5,000 万人になると予想されている。

　そのような状況にあって**人工知能（AI: artificial intelligence）**を備えたロボットが、**人口減少社会（declining population）**を支える**労働力（labor force）**として期待されている。そして、**自動運転車（autonomous car）**はその代表例である。信頼性の高い自動運転車が実用化されれば、例えば、今問題となっている運送業界の人手不足が解消されることは、容易に想像できる。

　しかしながら、自動運転技術の発展だけでは、その実用化は達成されない。道路や信号といったインフラをはじめとする社会全体の環境が、自動運転車に合わせて最適化される必要がある。とりわけ先進諸国では、自動車を取り巻く産業全体への経済的影響を無視するわけにはいかず、さらには事故が発生した場合の法的責任の所在を明確化する必要があるなど、検討すべき課題は多岐にわたる。そうしたことから、先進諸国での急激な変化は難しいのではないか、という見方もある。携帯電話の普及がそうであったように、自動運転車に合わせた環境を整備する上で制約が少ない**開発途上国（developing countries）**がその実用化の先鞭を付けることになるかもしれない。

▶ 本文出典
　イギリスの雑誌 *The Economist* の 2015 年 6 月第 1 週号に掲載された記事を一部改変したもの。

▶ pod
　pod はもともと「（マメ科植物の種子が入っている殻である）さや」の意味だが、文中で紹介されている pod は、ロンドンのヒースロー空港内を移動する新交通システム Heathrow Pod で使われている、カプセル状の乗り物のこと。乗客 4 人とその荷物を運ぶ空港内の新しい移動手段で、旅客ターミナルと駐車場の間を時速約 40 キロメートルで移動する。運転手が存在せず、バッテリーに充電された電気を動力源としていることから、次世代の乗り物として注目されている。

▶ touchscreen kiosk
　コンビニエンスストアなどに設置されている、オンラインシステムによる通信機能をもつ情報端末のこと。タッチパネル式のディスプレイを備えており、各種チケットの販売や公共料金の支払い、デジタル写真プリントなどのサービスを提供している。

▶ road capacity
　道路［交通］容量。ある道路が何台の自動車を通過させることができるかという、その道路が構造上有している能力のこと。1 時間に通過できる自動車の最大数である「時間交通容量」を指すことが多い。

Chapter 12

テーマ解説

人工知能（AI: artificial intelligence）の発展による**技術的失業（technological unemployment）**の懸念は、2013 年にオックスフォード大学のマイケル・A・オズボーン准教授とカール・ベネディクト・フライ博士が著した論文 *The Future of Employment*（邦訳：雇用の未来）に端を発する。彼らは 702 種にもおよぶ職種を研究対象とし、「今後 10 〜 20 年でアメリカの雇用者の約 47% が仕事の**自動化（automation）**により職を失う危険性がある」と結論付けた。取って代わられる可能性が高い職種として、工場労働者、タクシーやトラックの運転手などがよく挙げられるが、所謂**ホワイトカラー（white collar）**と呼ばれる会計士や弁護士の助手などの知的労働者も、職を奪われる可能性が高いとされている。一方で、建築家やデザイナーなど、独創性が求められる職種はその可能性がかなり低いと予測されている。

対して、**経済協力開発機構（the Organization for Economic Cooperation and Development：OECD）**が 2016 年に発表した研究結果では、「21 の OECD 加盟国において、将来自動化される仕事の割合は 9% に留まり、技術的進歩による脅威は考えられているものよりもかなり低い」と予測されている。

アメリカの大手 IT サービス企業、コグニザントが 2017 年に出版した『*What to Do When Machines Do Everything*』では、AI の発展により新たに生まれる仕事として、会話や散歩の相手、サイバー都市の管理者、人間と機械からなる労働チームの責任者など、これまで想像もされなかったような職種が挙げられている。

▶ 本文出典
大学によるオリジナル英文。

▶ the first industrial revolution
第一次産業革命。一般的には、軽工業における機械の導入と石炭をエネルギー源としていた時期を指す。18 世紀半ばから 19 世紀のイギリスに端を発し、ハーグリーヴズやアークライトが発明した紡績機や、ワットによる蒸気機関が有名。蒸気機関技術は蒸気船や蒸気機関車の発明へと繋がり、同時に交通革命をもたらした。

▶ Luddite
ラッダイト、またはラダイトとも。第一次産業革命がもたらした機械化によって自分たちの職が奪われることをおそれ、19 世紀初頭に機械の破壊活動を行った手工業を中心とする労働者たちのこと。1799 年に織機を破壊した、Ned Ludd という労働者の名前が由来とされている。現代社会において、IT 技術の進歩が人々の仕事を奪うとする考え方のことを、当時のラッダイトにかけて「ネオ・ラッダイト」と呼ぶ。

▶ the second industrial revolution
第二次産業革命。19 世紀後半のドイツとアメリカを中心とした、重工業（鉄鋼、機械）の技術革命を指す。石油資源の利用によるガソリンエンジンの発明や、エジソンによる電気の発明が特徴とされ、自動車や飛行機の開発が進んだのもこの段階である。

▶ the third industrial revolution
第三次産業革命。「デジタル革命」とも呼ばれ、20 世紀後半からのコンピュータ利用や、インターネット技術の発達などに代表される。

▶ the fourth industrial revolution
第四次産業革命。ロボット工学や人工知能ならびに、IoT（Internet of Things「モノのインターネット」）、仮想現実、量子コンピュータ、自動運転車、ナノテクノロジーなど様々な分野における新興の技術革新が特徴。昨今、機械化による大量失業に焦点があてられることが多いが、将来、我々の人体においても機械化が進み、最終的には「ポストヒューマン」と呼ばれる「到底人間とは思えない人間」が台頭する時代が来ると考える者もいる。

▶ OECD(the Organization for Economic Cooperation and Development)
経済協力開発機構。1700 名以上の専門家を抱える世界最大のシンクタンクであり、国際経済分野において幅広い活動を行う国際機関。パリに本部を置き、世界 36 ヵ国が加盟している。

Chapter 13

テーマ解説

　動物の行動は、**走性（taxis）**（動物が光や熱など
の**刺激（stimulus）**に向かって運動を起こす性質、
例えば虫が夜間の街灯に集まる性質）や**反射
（reflex）**、さらにそれらが複雑に組み合わさった本
能行動である**先天的［生得的］行動（unlearned
behavior）**と、経験や学習によって形成される**後天
的［習得的］行動（acquired behavior）**に分けられる。
動物行動学（ethology）は、行動を先天的なものと
後天的なものに分けて、その発生原因を解明する学
問である。

　動物行動学における研究手法の１つに、動物が報
酬を最大化するために学習していく過程を観察する
ものがある。例えば、特定の行動をとるとエサがも
らえる状況を作り、動物が試行錯誤しながらエサが
手に入る規則に気づくまでの過程を観察するといっ
たものである。**哺乳類（mammal）**などの高等生物は、
学習によって報酬が得られる行動をとれることが分
かっているが、こうした研究によって得られた知見
は、**人工知能（artificial intelligence, AI）**の開発に
も大きく寄与している。人工知能の一形態である**強
化学習（reinforcement learning）**は、成果が最も
多く得られる方法を機械自身が学習するものだが、
その開発に動物の学習メカニズムの知見が影響を与
えているのだ。これは、科学がその分野だけでなく、
一見無関係だと思われる他の分野の発展にも貢献し
ていることを示す一例である。

▶ 本文出典
Gerd Gigerenzer, *Gut Feelings: The Intelligence of the
Unconscious*, Viking, 2007 を一部抜粋、一部改変したもの。

▶ T-maze
　Ｔ型迷路。その名の通りＴ字の形をした単純な構造の迷
路で、ラットやマウスなどを対象とした実験で用いられる。
Ｔ字の下端を出発地点とし、進んだ先の分岐点で実験対象
が左右どちらを選ぶのかを調べる。

▶ maximizing
　最大化。複数の行動選択肢の中から、最も報
酬が多く得られる行動を一貫して取り続けるこ
と。例えば、当選確率60％のＡの箱と当選確率
40％のＢの箱のどちらか一方からくじを引く試行を10回繰り返す場合、10回連続して
Ａの箱からくじを引けば、報酬を得る確率が最も高くなる。
この10回全てＡの箱からくじを引く行動が「最大化」で
ある。

▶ probability matching
　確率マッチング。心理学の用語。動物に２つの選択肢の
どちらか一方を選ばせる実験で、「動物が各選択肢を選ぶ確
率」が「各選択肢の報酬が得られる確率」と一致する現象
のこと。報酬が得られる確率は増えないので合理的な行動
ではないが、一部の動物を用いた実験でこの現象が発生す
ることが確認されている。

▶ expectation
　期待値。確率論で用いられる言葉で、ある試行の結果か
ら得られる数値の平均値のこと。
（例）
　・くじの合計は100本
　・1,000円もらえる１等くじは10本
　・100円もらえる２等くじは40本
　・外れくじは50本
以下が「くじ１本あたりの金額の期待値140円」の計算式。
　1000円×10/100 ＋ 100円×40/100 ＋ 0円×50/100
　＝ 100円＋ 40円＋ 0円
　＝ 140円

▶ natural selection
　自然淘汰［自然選択］。「生物に偶発的に発生する突然変
異のうち生存環境に有利なものが生き残ることで、その種
の進化の方向性が決まる」という考え方。1859年にチャー
ルズ・ダーウィンによって提唱された。
　この考えを説明するとき、例としてキリンが取り上げら
れることが多い。
　・かつては首が長いキリン、首が短いキリンが存在していた
　・キリンの生存環境において、何らかの状況（例えば木の高
　　いところからしか食料が入手できない状況）が発生し、首
　　が短いキリンは生存できなくなった
　・結果として首が長いキリンだけが生き残った
　・その首の長さが遺伝され、その後は首が長いキリンだけが
　　存在するようになった

Chapter 14

テーマ解説

　温室効果ガス（greenhouse (effect) gases）とは、主に二酸化炭素（carbon dioxide: CO_2）やメタンガス（methane gas: CH_4）を含む 6 種類の気体を指す。これらの気体が地球温暖化の原因となるメカニズムは今や小学生でも知っているが、早期教育の必要が事態のひっ迫を感じさせる。

　近年では、気温上昇によるオーストラリアの大規模火災や砂漠化、シベリア北部のツンドラやキリマンジャロの万年雪の消失など、地球温暖化が与える悪影響の例については枚挙にいとまがない。

　米国や日本に代表される**先進国（developed countries）**が排出した温室効果ガスが世界中の地表を暖めて寒冷地の氷や雪を溶かし、結果、温室効果ガスをほとんど排出しない**発展途上国（developing countries）**のモルジブ（Maldives）やツバル（Tuvalu）は海面上昇によって国家存亡の危機に立たされている―というのが一般的な論調。ただし近年は、こうした情報を裏付けるデータの信憑性に疑いが持たれた事件が発生したこともあり、また、長いスパンで見れば地球は寒冷化しているとの情報もある。入試での論調も、ステレオタイプに決めつけてかからない方がいいかもしれない。

▶ **本文出典**

　2012 年 7 月 18 日のインターネット版 *Washington Post* に掲載された記事から採られたもので、タイトルは "Not so fast blaming global warming"「地球温暖化を責めるのはちょっと待とう」。

▶ **flood in Thailand**

　タイで 2011 年 7 月から 12 月にかけて発生した洪水。当初は河川上流の北部で洪水が広がり、10 月中旬からは首都バンコクを水没させるにまで及んだ。洪水の原因は 7 月の台風 8 号によるタイ北部および東北部へ多量の降雨だが、以降の 9、10 月の台風の上陸が事態を悪化させた。この洪水による死者は 400 人以上に達し、現地に進出していた日系企業も工場の閉鎖するなど大きな被害を受けた。不安定な政情が被害を拡大させたという側面が指摘されている。

▶ **El Niño**

　エル・ニーニョ現象。ペルー沿岸から太平洋東部の赤道付近の広い海域で、例年より海水温が高い状態が 1 年程度続く現象。はっきりとした原因は不明だが、この現象は異常気象を引き起こし、日本では冷夏、暖冬の傾向がみられる。

▶ **La Niña**

　ラ・ニーニャ現象。エル・ニーニョ現象とは対照的に、同海域で海水温が低い状態が続く現象のこと。日本では猛暑、寒冬の傾向がみられる。

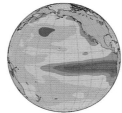 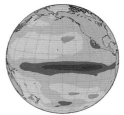

エル・ニーニョ発生時の海水温度　　　ラ・ニーニャ発生時の海水温度

▶ **stripping land**

　森林面積の増減は地域によって差があるが、世界的には減少傾向にある。2000 年から 2010 年にかけて全世界でほぼ四国と九州の合計と同じだけの森林面積が減少した。

▶ **hurricanes, as in New Orleans**

　アメリカ南東部を直撃したハリケーン（カトリーナ）で、特にルイジアナ州南部の都市ニューオーリンズに甚大な被害を及ぼした。2005 年 8 月 25 日にフロリダ半島を横断し、29 日にルイジアナ州に上陸し北上、ニューオーリンズ市域の約 8 割が水没した。

▶ **the historical record**

　古文書などに記された気象に関する記録や、木の年輪、氷河などを指す。記録によれば、平安時代や東山文化の頃は今よりも 0.5℃ 高い温暖な時期だったとされる。

▶ **more record-breaking heat events and fewer record-breaking cold ones**

　気象庁によれば、2013 年の 1 年間で、全世界で異常高温を記録した地点は延べ 823 箇所、異常低温を記録した地点は 340 箇所だった。ただし、異常高温に比べて異常低温がもたらす被害は甚大で、2003 年 1 月の異常寒波によってバングラディシュ、インド、ネパールで 1900 人が凍死し、2006 年の中国北西部の大雪では 100 万頭もの家畜が死んだと報告されている。

Chapter 15

テーマ解説

　近年メディアでよく取り上げられるキーワードの1つに「ビッグデータ」がある。いまだその明確な定義は定まっていないが、大まかに言えば「複雑で分類が困難な膨大な情報」のことである。この言葉が注目されたきっかけはGoogleの「**検索（search）**」である。検索した人の意図を「**予測（prediction）**」し、その意図に合っていると「予測」されるウェブサイトを返す作業に、彼らは数千億回に及ぶ過去の検索履歴データを**解析（analysis）**するプログラムを利用した。現在、多くの企業が膨大な情報を収集してそれを解析すれば、ビジネスに役立つ「予測」が入手できると考えている。店舗が発行するポイントカードは、「割引」をアピールしているだけではなく、客がいつ、何を購入したかの情報を収集するために発行しているのだ。

　これは、優れた商店主が日々行っていることと原理は同じである。彼らは季節や曜日、天候、周辺で行われるイベントなどのさまざまな情報に基づいて品揃えを日々変更する。過去の店の売上状況とそのときの非常に複雑な状況（情報）を把握し、それらを結びつけて（分類して）、未来を予測しているのだ。こうした能力は、過去に関する記憶力と、論理的かつ客観的な思考力が支えている。この「過去に関する記憶」を「ビッグデータ」に置き換えるとわかりやすい。そして「論理的かつ客観的な思考力」に置き換わるのは、**統計学（statistics）**である。統計学が行う作業は、条件に合うサンプルを抽出し、そこで得た複雑な情報間の関係性を発見することだが、これまでは限られた情報でしかできなかったことが、コンピューターの高性能化によって、膨大なデータを扱えるようになったのだ。近年、書店では「統計学のコーナーを設ければ売上げが上がる」と言われているようだが、今後ますます統計学が注目されることは間違いないだろう。

▶ **本文出典**

　英国の科学雑誌 *New Scientist magazine* の 2013 年 3 月 16 日号に掲載された、"What your Facebook 'likes' really say about you" を一部改変したもの。

　コジンスキ氏による研究論文は、米国科学アカデミーが発行する機関紙 *Proceedings of the National Academy of Sciences of the United States of America(PNAS)*（米国科学アカデミー紀要）の 2013 年 3 月 9 日号に "Private traits and attributes are predictable from digital records of human behavior" のタイトルで掲載されている。

▶ **Facebook**

　フェイスブック。世界最大のソーシャル・ネットワーキング・サービス（SNS）。2004 年、ハーバード大学の学生だったマーク・ザッカーバーグ氏を中心に設立された。

▶ **machine-learning**

　コンピューター学習。機械学習とも呼ばれる。人工知能（AI）の一種で、人間が学習するのと同様に、コンピューターに学習機能を持たせる技術。

▶ **model**

　モデル。さまざまな要素の関係を定式化して表したもの。本文中の their model は、情報を組み合わせた膨大なデータから本質的な規則性を抽出した「解析モデル（analysis model）」のことだと思われる。新たなサンプルを分類するときには、この規則性を基にして予測される。

▶ **Democrats and Republicans**

　民主党と共和党。米国は典型的な 2 大政党制の国であり、1853 年に就任した第 14 代大統領フランクリン・ピアース以降の大統領はすべてこの両党から選出されている。支持基盤は、リベラル政党である民主党が労働者や有色人種、保守政党の共和党は富裕層、南部・中西部の白人である。この両党以外の党はすべてまとめて第 3 党（Third party）と呼ばれる。

Chapter 16

テーマ解説

　正確ではない情報は、社会に悪影響を与える。当然、そうした情報の中で最も悪質なものは、詐欺などを目的とする悪意ある情報である。しかし、良心を発端とする情報が社会に悪影響を与えることも多い。

　流言（rumor）に関する研究でよく取り上げられる例として、1973年の豊川信用金庫事件がある。通学途中の高校生が列車内で発した「信用金庫は危ないよ」という言葉が、「豊川信用金庫が破綻する」という流言に発展し、5日間で約20億円の預金が引き出される取り付け騒ぎを引き起こした。きっかけは信用金庫に就職が決まった高校生に対して、その友人が「（銀行強盗が入るかもしれないから）危ないよ」とからかったことだったが、それが流言に発展した原因も悪意によるものではなかった。調査記録によれば、初期の段階で「早く預金を引き出したほうがいい」と20人以上の顧客に電話した商店主や、無線を使って広く情報を拡散した人物がいた。しかし、そうした流言を拡散した人々の行動の動機は、社会の混乱を目的としたものでも、豊川信用金庫を標的にしたものでもなく、大半は「知人への親切心」だったのである。

　正確な情報を発信するためには専門的な**知見（knowledge）**や調査が必要であり、情報を選び出す作業にも一定の調査は必要である。インターネットによって、かつては「希少な」資源だった正しい情報は、誰でも入手できる「安価な」資源になりつつある。しかし、その中には悪意ある情報だけでなく、悪意のない、**誤解（misunderstanding）**や思い込みによる情報も大量に含まれている。とりわけ人間が冷静さを失いがちな災害時などの危機的な状況においては、誤解や思い込みが発生しやすくなり、人間の良心が原動力となって、不正確な情報が溢れることになる。そうした現象は今後も十分起こりうることなので、情報は、その発信と受信には一定の知識と調査が必要なものであり、扱いには注意を要するものであることを強く認識する必要がある。

▶ **本文出典**

　Ann Banham, *"The Myth of Nonverbal Communication,"*, Toastmaster, March 2013 を一部改変したもの。

▶ **nonverbal communication**

　非言語メッセージ。言葉以外のメッセージのことを指し、非言語コミュニケーションとも呼ばれる。チャールズ・ダーウィンの『The Expression of Emotions in Man and Animals』（邦題『人及び動物の表情について』）（1872）における研究が最初とされている。非言語メッセージの例は幅広く、「表情」「顔色」「視線」「声のトーン」「話す速さ」「身振り手振り」から、「服装」「髪型」「スキンシップの有無」「聞き手との距離の取り方」「呼吸の深さ」にまで及ぶ。

▶ **Albert Mehrabian**

　アルバート・メラビアン（1939 -）。カリフォルニア大学ロサンゼルス校（UCLA）心理学名誉教授。言語によ

るメッセージと非言語メッセージのどちらが相対的に重要かの研究をし、それらをまとめた著書『Silent Messages』で注目された。その研究結果は「メラビアンの法則」、「7-38-55のルール」などと呼ばれ、コミュニケーションスキルに関するセミナーなどで誤って引用されてきた。

▶ *Silent Messages*

　1971年のアルバート・メラビアンの著書。メラビアンは、面と向かったコミュニケーションは「言葉」「声の調子」「非言語的な行動・態度」の3つの要素からなると定義し、それぞれの要素間に矛盾があった場合、例えば、暗く沈んだ表情で「あなたを怒ってない」と言ったときなどに、聞き手は「言葉」からの情報を7%、「声の調子」からの情報を38%、「非言語的な行動や態度」からの情報を55%の割合で受け取る、と結論づけた。ただし、この法則は限定的な状況でのみ成り立つものであり、感情などの要素を含まない単純な事実の伝達が行われる状況などにおいては適用されない、としている。

Chapter 17

テーマ解説

地球の起源は約45億年前だと考えられている。直径10kmほどの**微惑星（planetesimal）**が衝突を繰り返し、それらが結合して地球になった。当時の地表は、衝突で発生する熱による高温のマグマであった。次第に衝突する微惑星の数が減ったため地表は冷却されて、地球は岩石の惑星となった。

地球の誕生当時、大気中には微惑星の衝突によって放出された大量の**水蒸気（moisture）**と**二酸化炭素（carbon dioxide）**が存在していた。それらは**温室効果（greenhouse effect）**をもたらし、誕生当時の地表の温度は1000℃を超えていた。その後、微惑星の衝突が減少して徐々に地球の温度が下がり始めると、大気中の水蒸気は雨となって地表に降り注ぎ、やがて海洋を形成した。大気中にあった大量の二酸化炭素が海に吸収されたことによって温室効果は減退し、地球の温度はさらに低下した。

他の惑星に生命体が存在する条件としては、我々人間を含む地球上の生命体の基礎となっている**炭素（carbon）**、そして液体の水、**重力（gravity）**から生命体を守る岩石の地表が必要だと考えられている。地球外生命体の可能性を探る研究の基本的な考え方は、先の条件を満たす惑星を探索することである。しかし、「木星のような、地表も液体の水も存在しないガス状の惑星に、風船のように浮遊する生命体」が存在する可能性を検討している科学者もいる。それほど宇宙に関しては未解明な部分が多いのである。

▶ 本文出典

本英文は2011年9月14日付の米国の週刊誌 *TIME FOR KIDS* の記事 "Another Earth? — Scientists may have discovered the most earthlike planet yet."「もう1つの地球？─ 科学者たちはこれまでで最も地球に似た惑星を発見したのかもしれない」から採られている。

▶ rocky place

天体に生命が存在するための条件の1つは、その天体が岩石質で陸地があることである。水星、金星、地球、火星の四つの地球型惑星は岩石質で、陸地がある。木星、土星、天王星、海王星の木星型惑星はガスで出来ており、生命が存在するには難しい環境だと考えられている。

▶ habitable zone

ハビタブルゾーン。太陽系では金星から火星までがその領域にあたり、地球はその中心に位置している。

▶ Goldilocks

ゴルディロックス。本文では HD85512b と呼ばれる惑星を指しているが、天体用語としては、ハビタブルゾーン内にあり、かつ生命体の進化に適した環境を長期間維持している領域のことを指す場合もある。

▶ constellation Vela

帆座。アルゴ座を4分割したうちの1つ。日本からは1〜4月の南天の低い位置にその一部を見ることができる。

▶ Kepler space mission

ケプラー探査。NASA が太陽系外の惑星を見つけるために2009年にケプラー宇宙望遠鏡を打ち上げたプロジェクト。はくちょう座とこと座近くの15万ほどの恒星を観測している。2012年2月までに2321の惑星候補を発見し、後の追観測によって77が惑星であると確認された。

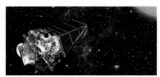

ケプラー探査機

▶ the Milky Way galaxy

天の川銀河（銀河系）。太陽系が属する銀河の名称。銀河とは、恒星系や宇宙塵、実態不明なダークマターなどが重力によって拘束された天体のこと。観測可能な宇宙にある銀河の総数は7兆を超えるとも言われている。天の川銀河の直径は約10万光年で、恒星が約1千億、地球と同程度の惑星が少なくとも170億は存在していると考えられている。夜の空で光の帯状に見える「天の川」は、（地球もその内部にあるので）天の川銀河を内側から見たものである。

▶ HARPS

南米チリのアタカマ砂漠のラ・シラ天文台に設置された太陽系外惑星を発見するための高解像度の分光器を備えた専用望遠鏡。惑星が恒星を公転する時の引力の作用が、恒星が発する光に波長の偏りを発生させる。その偏りを感知することで、惑星の存在を確認する。

ラ・シラ天文台の望遠鏡

Chapter 18

テーマ解説

バイアス（bias）とは、ある物事に対する偏った見方のことを意味する。バイアスには様々な種類が存在するが、それらを包括的に表した言葉が「**認知バイアス（cognitive bias）**」である。認知バイアスとは、人が何かを判断する際に、自身の考えや周囲の環境など多種多様な要因によって歪んだ決定を下してしまうことを指し、人間が犯しうる認知上の基本的な誤りのことを言う。

日々の生活を送る上で、我々が認知バイアスの影響を受けないようにすることは不可能に近い。本文に出てきた**確証バイアス（confirmation bias）**も認知バイアスの一種であるが、他にも、自己の感情に影響を受けて判断を歪ませてしまう**感情バイアス（emotional bias）**、成功の要因は自分にあるとし、失敗の原因をすべて自分以外の他人や周囲の環境にあるとしてしまう**自己奉仕バイアス（self-serving bias）**、自然災害などに対して「自分だけは大丈夫」だと考えてしまう**正常性バイアス（normalcy bias）**、物事が過ぎ去った後からまるでそれが予測可能であったかのように振舞う**後知恵バイアス（hindsight bias）**など、枚挙に暇がないほど多くの心理学上の分類がなされている。

▶ 本文出典
大学によるオリジナル英文。

▶ Peter Wason
ピーター・ウェイソン（1924-2003）。1953年にオックスフォード大学で心理学の修士号を、1956年にユニヴァーシティ・カレッジ・ロンドン（UCL）にて博士号を取得。1980年代初頭に引退するまで、UCLで認知心理学者として教鞭をとり、「確証バイアス」という言葉を造り出した。

ウェイソンは、本文に登場した「2-4-6問題」の他にも様々な認知心理学に関する実験を行っているが、中でも1966年に自らが考案した「ウェイソン選択課題（Wason selection task）」という論理パズルが有名。

★★

「ウェイソン選択課題［4枚カード問題］」の例

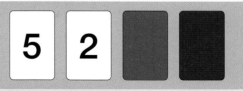

■ 設定（上図参照）
片面に数字が描かれ、その裏面には色が塗られた4枚のカードがあり、2枚のカードは数字が見える状態で、残りの2枚は色が塗られた面が見える状態で置かれている。

■ 問題
「偶数が描かれたカードの裏面は赤である」という仮説の正誤を確認するためには、どのカードを裏返してその裏面を確認する必要があるか」

この問に答えるために、各カード毎の「裏返す必要の有無」を、以下に整理してみよう。

「5」のカード：裏が何色であっても仮説の正誤は証明できない（「奇数」の裏が「赤」であっても仮説が誤りであることにはならない）。よって裏返す必要はない。

「2」のカード：裏が「青」の場合は、仮説の誤りを証明できる。よって裏返す必要がある。裏が「赤」だった場合、仮説の正しさは確認できる。

「赤」のカード：裏が「奇数」の場合でも、仮説の誤りを証明できない（「奇数」の裏が「赤」でも仮説が誤りであることにならない）。裏が「偶数」の場合、仮説の正しさは確認できるが、その証明にはならない。よって、必ずしも裏返す必要はない。

「青」のカード：裏が「偶数」だった場合、仮説の誤りを証明できる。よって裏返す必要がある。

以上より、解答は、「『2』のカード」と「『青色』のカード」の2枚である。

ウェイソンが行った実験における正答率は10%にも満たず、多くの被験者は「『2』のカードと、『赤』のカードの2枚を裏返して確認する必要がある」と答えた。彼は、この回答のような「仮説の正しさを確認する証拠を探すだけで、仮説の誤りを証明しようとしない傾向」を、確証バイアスの影響であると考えた。

★★

Cutting Edge
Blue

定価 700 円＋税

初刷発行：2024 年 10 月 25 日

編著者：池上　博

株式会社 エミル出版

〒102-0072　東京都千代田区飯田橋 2-8-1
TEL 03-6272-5481　FAX 03-6272-5482
ISBN978-4-86449-140-2 C7082

Cutting Edge

Blue

Navi Book

Chapter 1: *For the first time ...*

Chapter 3: *A study suggests ...*

Chapter 10: *"Organic": in less ...*

Chapter 11: *The spread of ...*

Chapter 14: *Can you blame ...*

Chapter 17: *Since the start ...*

ÉMILE

◆ 【語句】

　意味が空欄になっているものは、すべて入試必出の「重要語句」です。分からなければ辞書を引いて、覚えるまで何度も確認しましょう。

　音声ダウンロードを活用して、語句の正しい発音を確認しましょう。聞き流しながら語句の意味が確認できるように、音声は「英語→日本語（の意味）」の順で収録されています。

◆ 【本文解説】

　入試頻出の、少し分かりにくい構文、文構造を解説しています。難しいと感じた文については、問題を全て解いたあとでこの解説を読んで確認しましょう。また、参考書や辞書で検索しやすいように見出しをつけていますので、理解できるまで、自分で調べることが大切です。この「じっくりと読んで理解する」作業を怠ると、学習効果は半減します。粘り強く繰り返すことで、知らず知らずのうちに「読める」ようになるのです。

◆ 【段落要旨・百字要約】

　各段落ごとの要旨を完成させて、百字要約につなげる演習をします。この演習を繰り返すことで、国公立大の二次試験で問われる「要約力」「記述力」を効率的に養うことができます。

　やみくもに「書く」ことを繰り返しても、要約する力は身につきません。要約文を完成させるためには、「必要な情報と不必要な情報の選別」と「必要な情報をつなぎ合わせること」に慣れる必要があります。ここではその2点を意識しながら演習できるように構成されています。

● 目次 ●

Chapter	1	「教育と疾病」	東京理科大	2
Chapter	2	「最後のメッセージ」	明治学院大	6
Chapter	3	「目の大きさと脳の関係」	岡山大	10
Chapter	4	「液体燃料問題」	鹿児島大	14
Chapter	5	「貴重な教訓」	関西学院大	18
Chapter	6	「コーク VS ペプシ」	宮城大	22
Chapter	7	「動物の社会的距離」	北里大	26
Chapter	8	「睡眠の役割」	三重大	30
Chapter	9	「口論と真実」	愛知教育大	34
Chapter	10	「オーガニック」	名古屋市立大	38
Chapter	11	「自動運転車」	法政大	44
Chapter	12	「AI と仕事」	滋賀県立大	48
Chapter	13	「行動の背景」	弘前大	54
Chapter	14	「災害と温暖化」	広島大	58
Chapter	15	「ビッグデータ」	法政大	62
Chapter	16	「『事実』なるもの」	岩手大	66
Chapter	17	「ハビタブルゾーン」	西南学院大	70
Chapter	18	「確証バイアス」	北海道大	74
Vocabulary Building Drill　語句確認ドリル				80

For the first time in history, a major disease might soon be eliminated without the use of drugs. The Carter Center, an organization run by former US President Jimmy Carter, has predicted that the Guinea worm* disease will be the first parasitic disease to be (1)eradicated and the first disease to be (1)eradicated without the use of vaccines or medical treatment. The Guinea worm is (2)a parasite, which is an organism or creature that lives on or in another organism or creature. People get Guinea worm disease by drinking dirty, contaminated water. After drinking contaminated water, the worms grow in the body for about a year. Once they have grown, they emerge slowly from the body often around the foot area. It can take weeks for the worm to fully emerge. And during this time, the victim is in great pain, making it almost impossible for the victim to work, move around or go about their lives.

But the Guinea worm can now only be found in a few African countries, thanks to a 22-year fight against the disease led by the Carter Center. Carter was moved when he saw its victims in Africa. "It was a horrible disease, almost indescribably bad. It was an ancient disease and it didn't seem to have any solution. (3)It was almost an impossible problem, so that's why we decided to try to solve it."

The strategy to eliminate this disease has been consistent: (4)public education. Previously, villagers thought the disease came from witchcraft, or from eating bad meat. (　5　), now they know that it comes from the ponds, where they get their drinking water. This disease has tormented villagers for thousands of years and it will soon be eliminated by educating the villagers and teaching them to use very simple water filters. In 1986, there were an estimated 3.5 million cases of Guinea worm in 21 countries in Africa and Asia. In 2012, there were only 512 documented cases in four countries in sub-Saharan Africa. The Carter Center, along with the US chemical company Dupont, developed a fine cloth filter which was effective and could be made and distributed cheaply. (6)By filtering all the village drinking water through these fine cloths, the villagers were able to stop the worms from entering the human body.

　　* Guinea worm「ギニア虫」

❶

❷

❸

❹

❺

❻

❼

語句　音声は、「英語」→「日本語の意味」の順で読まれます。　　　　CD 1 - Tr 4 ～ 7

入試基本レベル

1 **major** [méidʒər]

2 **organization** [ɔ̀ːrɡənəzéiʃən]

3 **disease** [dizíːz]

6 **get a disease**

10 **victim** [víktim]

12 **thanks to ～**

13 **be moved**

15 **ancient** [éinʃənt]

24 **along with ～**

25 **cloth** [klɔ́(ː)θ]

25 **effective** [iféktiv]

27 **stop A from** *doing*

入試標準レベル（共通テスト・私大）

1 **eliminate** [ilímənèit]

2 **former** [fɔ́ːrmər]

3 **predict** [pridíkt]

4 **vaccine** [væksíːn]

5 **medical treatment**

5 **organism** [ɔ́ːrɡənìzm]

6 **creature** [kríːtʃər]

8 **emerge** [imə́ːrdʒ]

9 **fully** [fúli]

10 **be in (great) pain**

11 **go about ～**

14 **horrible** [hɔ́rəbl]（形）

15 **solution** [səlúːʃən]

17 **strategy** [strǽtədʒi]

17 **consistent** [kənsístənt]

18 **previously** [príːviəsli]

18 **come from ～**　～から来る、～が原因である

22 **estimated** [éstəmèitid]

22 **case** [kéis]（名）　症例

23 **document** [dάkjəmènt]（動）

24 **chemical** [kémikl]

25 **fine** [fáin]（形）　きめの細かい

26 **distribute** [distríbjət]

入試発展レベル（二次・有名私大）

3 **parasitic** [pæ̀rəsítik]

5 **parasite** [pǽrəsàit]

7 **contaminated** [kəntǽminèitid]

20 **torment** [tɔːrmént]

22 **filter** [fíltər]（名）

26 **filter** [fíltər]（動）

その他

4 **eradicate** [irǽdikèit]　～を全滅させる、～を撲滅する

14 **indescribably** [ìndiskráibəbli]

　言葉で言い表せないほど

18 **witchcraft** [wítʃkræ̀ft]　魔法、魔術

24 **sub-Saharan Africa**　サハラ砂漠以南のアフリカ

本文解説

1 【同格表現】【不定詞の形容詞的用法】

(l.2) (S)<u>**The Carter Center**</u>, **an organization run by former US President Jimmy Carter**, (V)<u>**has predicted**</u> (O)<u>**that**</u> (S')<u>the Guinea worm disease</u> (V')<u>will be</u> (C'1)<u>the first parasitic disease **to be eradicated**</u> and (C'2)<u>the first disease **to be eradicated**</u> without the use of vaccines or medical treatment.

▶ an organization run by ... Jimmy Carter は、The Carter Center を補足説明している同格表現。この run は他動詞 run「～を運営する」の過去分詞で、an organization を修飾している。

▶ 全体の構造は、The Carter Center ... has predicted that ～「…であるカーター・センターは、～（ということ）を予測している」の SVO の文。has predicted の目的語は that 以下すべて。

▶ that 節内の主語は the Guinea worm disease で、述語動詞は will be、補語が the first disease ... and the first disease ... と 2 つ並列されている。

▶ the first parasitic disease to be ... は「…される最初の寄生虫症」。不定詞句は disease を修飾する形容詞の働きをしている。すぐ後の the first disease to be ... も同様に、不定詞句が disease を修飾している。

2 【関係代名詞の非制限用法】

(l.5) The Guinea worm is a parasite, **which** is an organism or creature that lives on or in another organism or creature.

▶ 関係代名詞 which 以下は、先行詞の a parasite「寄生虫」を補足説明している。

▶ lives on or in another organism の live に続く前置詞は on と in の 2 つ。この on は〈接触〉を表し「他の有機体または生物の体表（に付着した状態）で生存する」という意味で、句動詞の live on ～「～を食べて暮らす」ではないことに注意。

3 【分詞構文】【形式目的語】

(l.10) And during this time, the victim is in great pain, **making it almost impossible for the victim to work, move around or go about their lives.**

▶ この making は分詞構文で、意味上の主語は great pain。意味上の主語が文の主語（ここでは the victim）と異なる場合は意味上の主語を省略しないのが原則だが、ここでは文中のしかも直前に明示されているので省略されていると考えられる。

▶ making it almost impossible for the victim to work, ... は make it ～ to do「…することを～にする」の形式目的語構文。it は形式目的語で、真目的語は to work, move around or go about their lives。

▶ for the victim は to work, ... 以下の意味上の主語。「患者が働いたり…することをほぼ不可能にする」。

4 【by *doing*】【teach A to *do*】

(l.20) This disease has tormented villagers for thousands of years and it will soon be eliminated **by educating** the villagers and **teaching them to use** very simple water filters.

▶ by *doing* で「～することによって」。ここでは 2 つの動名詞 educating と teaching が並列されている。

▶ teach A to *do* は「A に～するよう教える」。them は the villagers を指している。

展開	段落	要旨
導入	1	（①　　　　　　　）症が（②　　　　　　）を使うことなく撲滅されるかもしれない。 （①　　　　　　　）症は（③　　　　　）された水を飲むことで発症する。（①　　　　　　　） が体内で成長し、足周辺に出現すると、感染者は強い痛みに襲われる。
展開①	2	（④　　　　　　　　　　）の主導による病気との闘いのおかげで、（①　　　　　　　）は あまり見られなくなった。
展開②	3	（①　　　　　　　）症を撲滅するための戦略は、（⑤　　　　　　　）である。村人たちに、池 や沼の水をフィルターでろ過して飲むように教えることで、症例数は劇的に減少した。

■　以下を参考にして、「段落要旨」の下線部分を中心にまとめてみよう。

　▶「導入」の内容（20〜30字）

　▶「展開②」の内容（70〜80字）

　▶ 字数に余裕があれば、「展開①」の内容を適宜追加してもよい。

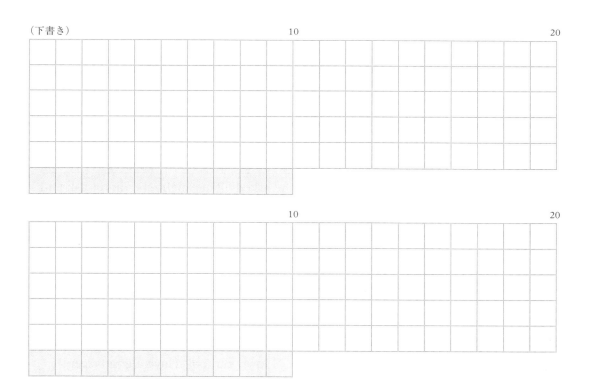

（下書き）

5

When I married my husband, six years ago, he already had four small children from his previous marriage. I became their stepmother, and watched them become young teenagers. Although they lived primarily with their mother, they spent a lot of time with us as well. Over the years, we all learned to adjust. We enjoyed vacations together, ate family meals, worked on homework, played baseball, rented videos. However, (1)<u>I continued to feel somewhat like an outsider.</u> Since I had no children of my own, my experience of parenting was limited to my husband's four, and often I felt sad because I would never know the special bond that exists between a parent and a child.

When the children moved to a town that was a five-hour drive away, my husband was understandably upset. We promptly set up an e-mail and chat-line service. (2)<u>This technology, combined with the telephone, would enable us to reach the children on a daily basis</u> by sending frequent notes and messages, and even chatting together when we were all on-line.

Ironically, these modern tools of communication can also be (3)<u>tools of alienation,</u> making us feel so out of touch, so much more in need of real human contact. If a computer message came addressed to "Dad", I'd feel forgotten and neglected. If my name appeared along with his, it would brighten my day and make me feel like I was part of (4)<u>their family unit</u> after all. Yet always there was some distance to be crossed, not just over the telephone wires.

Late one evening, as my husband slept in front of the television and I was catching up on my e-mail, an "instant message" appeared on the screen. It was from Margo, my oldest step-daughter, also up late and sitting in front of her computer five hours away. As usual, we sent several messages back and forth, exchanging the latest news. (5)<u>When we would "chat" like that, she wouldn't necessarily know if it was me or her dad operating the keyboard — that is unless she asked.</u> That night she didn't ask and I didn't identify myself either. After hearing the latest volleyball scores, the details about an upcoming dance at her school, and a history project she was working on, I commented that it was late and I should get to sleep. Her return message read, "Okay, talk to you later! Love you!"

As I read this message, a wave of sadness ran through me, as (6)<u>I realized that she must have thought she was writing to her father the whole time.</u> She and I would never have openly exchanged such words of affection. Feeling guilty for not clarifying, yet not wanting to embarrass her, I simply responded, "I love you too! Have a good sleep!"

I thought again of their family circle, that self-contained, private space where I was an outsider. I felt again the sharp ache of emptiness and otherness. Then, just as I was about to log off, Margo's final message appeared. It read, "Tell Dad good night for me too." With tear-filled, blurry eyes, I turned the computer off.

❶

❷ By ₁(   ) this technology together with the telephone, we would ₂(   ) ₃(   ) ₄(   ) reach the children every day.

❸
....

....

❹
....

❺
....

....

❻
....

❼
....

語句	音声は、「英語」→「日本語の意味」の順で読まれます。	CD 1 - Tr 14 〜 17

入試基本レベル

4 **as well** _____

11 **combine A with B** _____

11 **enable A to** *do* _____

33 **embarrass** [embǽrəs] _____

入試標準レベル（共通テスト・私大）

2 **previous** [príːviəs] _____

3 **primarily** [praimérli] _____

4 **adjust** [ədʒʌ́st] _____

5 **work on 〜** _____

6 **somewhat** [sʌ́mhwàt] _____

7 **be limited to** _____

8 **bond** [bánd]（名） _____

10 **promptly** [prámptli] _____

11 **on a daily basis** _____

12 **frequent** [fríːkwənt]（形） _____

15 **touch** [tʌ́tʃ]（名） （精神的）接触、連絡

15 **out of touch** _____

16 **address A to B** _____

16 **neglect** [niglékt]（動） _____

17 **brighten** [bráitn] _____

18 **unit** [júːnit] _____

20 **catch up on** _____

23 **back and forth** _____

23 **latest** [léitist] _____

25 **operate** [áprèit] _____

26 **identify** [aidéntəfài] _____

28 **comment** [káment]（動） _____

32 **guilty** [gílti] _____

35 **ache** [éik] _____

入試発展レベル（二次・有名私大）

10 **understandably** [ʌ̀ndərstǽndəbli] _____

14 **ironically** [airánikəli] _____

14 **alienation** [èiliənéiʃən] _____

27 **upcoming** [ʌ́pkʌ̀miŋ] _____

32 **clarify** [klǽrifài] _____

35 **emptiness** [émptinəs] _____

その他

7 **parent** [péərənt]（動） 親となる

34 **self-contained** 他を寄せつけない

35 **otherness** [ʌ́ðərnəs] 異質なこと

36 **log off** ログオフする

37 **blurry** [bláːri] ぼんやりとかすんだ

本文解説

1 【分詞構文】【無生物主語】

(l.10) **This technology, combined with the telephone**, would enable us to reach the children on a daily basis by sending frequent notes and messages, and even chatting together when we were all on-line.

- ▶ 全体の構造は This technology would enable us to reach the children 〜 by sending —and even chatting together when .... 「この技術は—を送ったり、…のときには一緒にチャットまでして、私たちが毎日子どもたちと連絡を取ることを可能にするだろう」。
- ▶ combined with the telephone は受動態の分詞構文。combine this technology with the telephone「この技術を電話と組み合わせる」が受動態になったものである。→「電話と組み合わされると」
- ▶ 主語がもの（= This technology）、目的語が人（= us）の無生物主語構文。目的語の人「私たちは」を主語にして、主語を副詞句として「この技術を使えば」のように訳すと日本語らしくなる。
  - *e.g.* The software enables you to access the Internet in seconds.
    「そのソフトはあなたが数秒でインターネットにアクセスすることを可能にする」
    →「そのソフトを使えば、数秒でインターネットにアクセスできる」
    = If you use the software, you can access the Internet in seconds.

2 【ironically：文修飾の副詞】【助動詞 can】【分詞構文】【使役動詞 make】

(l.14) **Ironically**, these modern tools of communication **can** also be tools of alienation, **making us feel so out of touch, so much more in need of real human contact.**

- ▶ ironically は文全体を修飾して「皮肉にも」の意。It is ironic that ... と表現することもできる。
- ▶ can は可能性を表し「〜することもある」。
- ▶ 分詞構文 making ... は and they make us feel ... と同意で、主語は these modern tools of communication「こうした現代のコミュニケーションの道具」（前の段落の an e-mail and chat-line service を指す）である。
- ▶ make us feel C で「私たちに C だと感じさせる」。C は so out of touch「人とのつながりがない」と、so much more in need of real human contact「ずっと多くの本当の人間的な接触を必要とする」の 2 つ。

3 【部分否定：not necessarily】

(l.24) When we would "chat" like that, she **wouldn't necessarily** know if **it was me or her dad operating the keyboard** — that is unless she asked.

- ▶ not necessarily は部分否定で「必ずしも〜でない」。
- ▶ it was me or her dad operating the keyboard は、it was me or her dad that[who] was operating the keyboard の that[who] was が省略されている、と考えられる。「キーボードを操作していたのは、私なのか、あるいはお父さんなのか」の意味。

展開	段落	要旨
起	1	私は（①　　　　）人の子どもの継母となった。子どもたちと多くの時間を過ごしてきたが、（②　　　　）のような気持ちを感じていて、実の親子の絆はわからないだろうと思っていた。
承①	2	子どもたちが遠方に引っ越したので、彼らと連絡を取るために、（③　　　　）やチャットのサービスを導入した。
承②	3	（③　　　　）やチャットでも疎外感を感じることがあった。私は子どもたちとの間に隔たりがあると感じていた。
転①	4	ある晩、相手が自分だとはっきりさせずに（④　　　　）とチャットをしたが、その返事の中に「愛しているわ」という言葉があった。
転②	5	（④　　　　）は、私ではなく（⑤　　　　）とやりとりしているのだと感じ悲しくなった。
結	6	（④　　　　）の最後の返事には、（⑤　　　　）への伝言があった。先ほどの愛情に満ちた言葉が自分に対するものだとわかり、私は涙があふれた。

■　以下を参考にして、「段落要旨」の下線部分を中心にまとめてみよう。
▶「起」の内容（20 ～ 30 字）
▶「転①、②」、「結」の内容（70 ～ 80 字）
▶ 字数に余裕があれば、「承①、②」の内容を追加してもよい。

（下書き）　　　　　　　　　　　　　　　　　　10　　　　　　　　　　　　　　　　　　20

10　　　　　　　　　　　　　　　　　　20

(1)A study suggests that people who live at higher latitudes★ have larger eyes and more ability in their brains to deal with visual information compared with those living nearer the equator★. Researchers measured the brain volumes and eye sizes of 55 skulls kept at the Oxford University Museum of Natural History dating from the 19th century. The skulls represented 12 different populations from around the world, including native people from England, Australia, China, Kenya, Micronesia and Scandinavia.

"As you move away from the equator, there's less and less light available, so humans have had to evolve bigger and bigger eyes," said (2)Ellie Pearce, a graduate student from Oxford University and the lead author on the study. "Their brains also need to be bigger to deal with the extra visual input. Having bigger brains doesn't mean that higher-latitude humans are (A); it just means they need bigger brains to be able to see well where they live." This suggests that someone from Greenland and someone from Kenya will have the same ability to detect detail, but the person from the higher latitude needs more brainpower and bigger eyes to deal with the lower light levels.

Professor Robin Dunbar, also from Oxford University and a co-author of the study, said that people whose ancestors lived within the Arctic Circle★ have eyeballs 20% bigger than people whose ancestors lived near the equator. They have an associated increase in the size of the visual part of the brain, which previous studies have shown matches with the size of the eyeball. Brain volume increases with latitude: people living at high latitudes north and south of the equator have bigger brains than people living near the equator.

The results, published in the journal *Biology Letters*, showed that the biggest brains, averaging 1,484 milliliters, were from Scandinavia, while the smallest brains, around 1,200 milliliters, came from Micronesia. The average eye size was 27 milliliters in Scandinavia and 22 milliliters in Micronesia. Professor Dunbar concluded that the increase in brain volume must have evolved relatively recently in human history. He added, "It's only within the last 10,000 years or so that modern humans have occupied all latitudes right up to the Arctic Circle. So, (3)this is probably (4)a development that's happened within the last 10,000 years."

★ latitude「緯度」 equator「赤道」 Arctic Circle「北極圏」

1 (1) ....

....

(2) ....

....

2 ....

....

....

3 ....

4 ....

5 ....

....

6 (1) .... (2) ....

語句　音声は、「英語」→「日本語の意味」の順で読まれます。　CD 1 - Tr 22 ～ 25

入試基本レベル

2	ability [əbíləti]	
2	brain [bréin]	
2	compared with ～	
3	researcher [risə́:rtʃər]	
3	measure [méʒər]（動）	
7	available [əvéiləbl]	
10	extra [ékstrə]（形）	
13	detail [ditéil]	
17	ancestor [ǽnsestər]	
20	match with ～	
27	relatively [rélətivli]	
29	development [divéləpmənt]	

入試標準レベル（共通テスト・私大）

1	study [stʌ́di]（名）	
2	deal with ～	
2	visual [víʒul]	
3	volume [válju:m]	
4	date from ～	
5	represent [rèprizént]	
5	native [néitiv]	
7	move away from ～	

8	evolve [ivʌ́lv]	
8	graduate student	
9	lead author	
13	detect [ditékt]	
19	associated [əsóuʃièitid]	
24	average [ǽvəridʒ]（動）	
28	occupy [ákjəpài]	

入試発展レベル（二次・有名私大）

3	the equator	赤道
3	skull [skʌ́l]	
4	natural history	
5	population [pàpjəléiʃən]	（ある地域に住む）人々
16	co-author	
17	the Arctic Circle	北極圏
19	previous study	

その他

1	high latitudes	高緯度地方
6	Micronesia [màikrəní:ʒə]	ミクロネシア
10	visual input	視覚（入力）情報
14	brainpower [bréinpàuər]	脳の力、知力
17	eyeball [áibɔ̀:l]	眼球
24	milliliter [mílilì:tər]	ミリリットル
29	right up to ～	～に至るまで

本文解説

1 【文構造】【不定詞の形容詞的用法】【代名詞 those】

(l.1) A study suggests / that people (who live at higher latitudes) have larger eyes and more ability in their brains **to deal with** visual information / compared with **those** living nearer the equator.

▶ 全体は A study suggests that ... 「ある研究は…を示唆している」。
▶ people ... have larger eyes and more ability (in their brains) to — compared with ～の英文構造は、「…の人々は～と比べて、より大きな目と、—するより高い（脳の）能力を持っている」。
▶ to deal with ...は ability を修飾する不定詞の形容詞的用法で、「視覚情報を処理するための（能力）」。
▶ those living ... は those who live nearer the equator と同意で、those は「人々」の意。

2 【as】【比較級 less and less】

(l.7) **As** you move away from the equator, there's **less and less** light available, so humans have had to evolve bigger and bigger eyes, ...

▶ as は接続詞で「～につれて」の意。
▶ less and less light available「利用できる光がだんだん減る」。〈比較級＋and＋比較級〉で「だんだん～、ますます」。

3 【文構造】【不定詞の形容詞的用法】【不定詞の副詞的用法】

(l.12) This suggests / that someone (from Greenland and someone from Kenya) will have the same ability (**to detect** detail), but the person (from the higher latitude) needs more brainpower and bigger eyes / **to deal with** the lower light levels.

▶ This は、第 2 段落第 1 文から直前の文までの内容「光の少ないところで視覚情報を処理するためには大きな脳や目が必要だが、そのぶん頭がいいわけではないこと」を指している。
▶ that 節内は、someone ... will have the same ability (to ～), but the person ... need more ～「…の人は（～する）同じ能力があるだろうが、…の人はより～が必要だ」。will は推量。
▶ to detect detail は ability を修飾する不定詞の形容詞的用法。
▶ to deal with ～は目的を表す不定詞の副詞的用法で、「～に対処するために」。

4 【関係代名詞の非制限用法】【関係代名詞節中の挿入】

(l.18) They have an associated increase in the size of the visual part of the brain, **which previous studies have shown** matches with the size of the eyeball.

▶ an associated increase は「関連した増加」。
▶ , which は the size of ... the brain を先行詞とする、関係代名詞の非制限用法。
▶ previous studies have shown は関係代名詞の直後に挿入され、「過去の研究が示しているように」。挿入を省くと、which matches with ～「（脳の視覚部分の広さは）眼球の大きさに対応する」となる。

5 【強調構文】【副詞 right】

(l.28) **It's** only within the last 10,000 years or so **that** modern humans have occupied all latitudes **right** up to the Arctic Circle.

▶ It is ～ that ... の強調構文で、「…したのは過去 1 万年ほどの間のことでしかない」。
▶ right は副詞で、up to を強めている。「～までずっと」の意。

展開	段落	要旨
総論	1	ある研究によると、（①　　　　　　　　）地方に住む人は、（②　　　　　　　　）付近に住む人に比べて大きな目を持ち、視覚情報を処理する脳の能力が高い。
本論①	2	（①　　　　　　　　）地方では得られる（③　　　　　）の量が減るため、より大きな目を発達させる必要があった。そして、脳も新たな視覚情報を処理するために、より大きくなる必要があった。
本論②	3	祖先が（①　　　　　　　　）に住んでいた人は、眼球が大きい。さらに、（①　　　　　　　　）に住む人々は、（②　　　　　）付近に住む人々よりも大きな脳を持っている。
本論③	4	脳の容積の増加は、過去（④　　　　　　　）年ほどの間で起きた進化だと思われる。

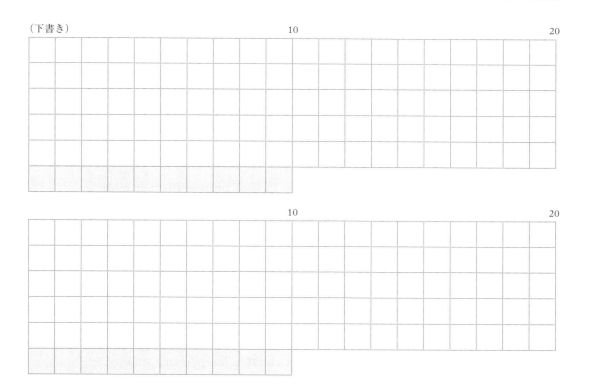

- ■　以下を参考にして、「段落要旨」の下線部分を中心にまとめてみよう。
  - ▶「総論」の内容（55〜65字）
  - ▶「本論①、③」の内容（35〜45字）
    【記述例】：「それ（＝「総論」）は〜のためであり、…の間に進化したものだ」
  - ▶「本論②」については、「本論①」とほぼ同じ内容のためここでは省略。

（下書き）

CD 1
🔊 26

I have a friend who likes to barbecue on his back deck. He puts charcoal in the grill, squirts★ some lighter fluid★ on the charcoal, and throws a match on it. The lighter fluid goes "BOOM," but somehow his charcoal never starts burning. So he squirts more lighter fluid, lights another match, and watches it blow up again while his wife and I make fun of him. He makes frequent trips to the store for more lighter fluid. (1)One day his wife commented, "Charlie's charcoal grill runs on lighter fluid."

In a way, muscle is like that grill. Muscle burns both fat and sugar: the sugar burns instantly like lighter fluid, yielding only a small amount of energy, but the fat continues to burn for a long, long time, like charcoal (A). You get lots more calories, or energy, from a fat molecule★ than you do from a sugar molecule. When you're playing active sports you may run out of sugar; you never run out of fat.

We now know that even people who are starving never, never, never (B) all of their body fat. This may surprise you, since starving or anorexic★ people look so emaciated★, but there is fat even on the bodies of people who weigh only seventy-five pounds. They look like skeletons when they die because they lose so much muscle, but autopsies★ show that they still have ten or fifteen pounds of fat hidden inside. (2)These people do not, in fact, starve to death.

Nobody in the history of the earth has ever actually starved to death. (3)At some point during starvation, as the body runs out of glucose★ it starts using protein for fuel. In the process of burning protein, it taps★ the immune system antibodies★, which are proteins. Starving people become highly susceptible★ to bacteria and viruses; they die of infectious diseases precipitated★ by lack of protein in their bodies.

Like starving people, those who are very fit occasionally have (4)lighter-fluid problems. During long, rigorous sports events their muscles run out of sugar. (5)When that happens, their energy drops abruptly★ because the burning of fat, triggered by sugar's spark, has ceased. Athletes think they run out of energy because their sugar has run out, but in reality, they have plenty of "fat energy" left (C). They constantly look for ways to store more sugar in their muscles, mistakenly thinking that sugar is their primary fuel. But it is only the starter fluid; fat is the primary fuel.

* squirt「吹きかける」　lighter fluid「液体燃料」　molecule「分子」　anorexic「拒食症の」　emaciated「やせ衰えた」
autopsy「解剖」　glucose「ブドウ糖」　tap「資源として活用する」　immune system antibody「免疫系の抗体」
susceptible「影響されやすい」　precipitate「突然引き起こす」　abruptly「突然、不意に」

❶ ....

❷ (A) .... (B) .... (C) ....

❸

❹ ....
....

❺ ....

❻ ....
....

❼ ....

| 語句 | 音声は、「英語」→「日本語の意味」の順で読まれます。 | CD 1 - Tr 31 ～ 34 |

入試基本レベル

12 **active** [ǽktiv]

17 **hide** [háid]（動）

21 **fuel** [fjúːəl]（名）

23 **die of ～**

28 **plenty of ～**

入試標準レベル（共通テスト・私大）

3 **somehow** [sʌ́mhàu]

4 **blow up**

5 **make fun of ～**

5 **make a trip to ～**

5 **frequent** [fríːkwənt]（形）

6 **comment** [kάment]（動）

6 **run on ～**

8 **in a way**

8 **muscle** [mʌ́sl]

8 **fat** [fǽt]（名）

9 **instantly** [ínstntli]

9 **yield** [jíːld]（動）

12 **run out of ～**

13 **starve** [stάːrv]

15 **weigh** [wéi]

16 **skeleton** [skélətn]

20 **protein** [próutiːn]

22 **virus** [váirəs]

23 **infectious** [infékʃəs]

24 **occasionally** [əkéiʒnəli]

27 **cease** [síːs]

27 **athlete** [ǽθliːt]

28 **in reality**

28 **constantly** [kάnstntli]

29 **mistakenly** [mistéiknli]

30 **primary** [práimèri]

入試発展レベル（二次・有名私大）

1 **charcoal** [tʃάːrkòul]

2 **fluid** [flúːid]

21 **immune** [imjúːn]

25 **rigorous** [rígrəs]

26 **trigger** [trígər]（動）

27 **spark** [spάːrk]（名）

その他

1	**barbecue** [bάːrbikjùː]（動）	バーベキューをする
1	**deck** [dék]（名）	デッキ、テラス
2	**grill** [gríl]	グリル装置
3	**go boom**	ボンと音をたてる
3	**boom** [búːm]（名）	どーんと鳴る音
22	**bacteria** [bæktíəriə]	バクテリア
24	**fit** [fít]	健康な
26	**abruptly** [əbrʌ́ptli]	突然、不意に

本文解説

1 【時制：習慣を表す現在形】【make fun of】

(l.3) So he **squirts** more lighter fluid, **lights** another match, and **watches** it blow up again while his wife and I **make fun of** him.

- ▶ 現在形で記述されているのは、現在の習慣的な動作・反復的な出来事を表すため。
- ▶ 述語動詞は squirts / lights / watches の 3 つ。
- ▶ make fun of 〜「〜をからかう」 = ridicule

2 【コロン（:）】【分詞構文】【接続詞 but】

(l.8) Muscle burns both fat and sugar: the sugar burns instantly like lighter fluid, **yielding** only a small amount of energy, **but** the fat continues to burn for a long, long time, like charcoal （　A　）.

- ▶ : (colon「コロン」) は that is「つまり、すなわち」と同様の役割を果たす。コロン以下に前文のより詳しい説明を追加している。
- ▶ , yielding は分詞構文。= and it yields ...
- ▶ 接続詞 but は対比を表す指標。the sugar ... but the fat の対比に着目する。

3 【無生物主語】

(l.16) They look like skeletons when they die because they lose so much muscle, but **autopsies show that** they still have ten or fifteen pounds of fat hidden inside.

- ▶ autopsies show that ...「解剖は…ということを示している」→「解剖によって…だと示されている」

4 【受動態の分詞構文】【現在完了】

(l.25) When that happens, their energy drops abruptly because the burning of fat, **triggered by sugar's spark, has ceased.**

- ▶ triggered by sugar's spark は受動態の分詞構文。「〜によって引き起こされた」
- ▶ 「the burning of fat が止まったために〜する」という時間関係を明確にするために、現在完了形を用いている。

展開	段落	要旨
導入	1	友人がグリルの（①　　　　　）に（②　　　　　　　）を吹きかけてマッチを投げ入れるが、（②　　　　　　）だけが燃えてしまい、（①　　　　）は燃え始めない。
序論	2	筋肉は（③　　　　　）と（④　　　　　）を燃やす。（④　　　　）はすぐに燃えるが、わずかなエネルギーしか生まない。（③　　　　）は長く燃え、そこから多くのエネルギーが得られる。
本論①	3	飢えている人でも（③　　　　）の全てを使い果たすことはない。餓死したように見える人の体内にも（③　　　　）は残っている。
本論②	4	これまでに餓死した人は一人もいない。ブドウ糖を使い果たすと（⑤　　　　　　　）である免疫系の（⑥　　　　）を燃やし始め、その結果、感染症で亡くなるのだ。
結論	5	（④　　　　）を使い果たすと、残っている（③　　　　）の燃焼も止まる。そして（③　　　　）は残っているにもかかわらず、エネルギーが突然低下する。（④　　　　）は着火剤で（③　　　　）が主たる燃料なのである。

■　以下を参考にして、「段落要旨」の下線部分を中心にまとめてみよう。
　▶「導入」の内容は「具体的なエピソード」のため、省略。
　▶「序論」の内容（45 〜 55 字）
　▶「結論」の内容（50 〜 60 字）

（下書き）
　　　　　　　　　　　　　　　　　　　　10　　　　　　　　　　　　　　　　　20

　　　　　　　　　　　　　　　　　　　　10　　　　　　　　　　　　　　　　　20

CD 1
35

　　Last summer we watched a young boy build a sand castle at the beach.　He approached his task with the seriousness of a construction engineer working on a forty-story building.　He worked so hard gathering sand that after a half hour he had a large heap of it, which he then with great effort patted into a low building.　When he was finally satisfied with his work, he went over to his father.

　　"Look, Dad.　Look what I did."

36

　　The boy's father carefully studied the heap.　He walked around it as if inspecting a work of art.

　　"Charlie, you've made a great castle.　I think it's the best on the beach."

　　The boy's smile was as bright as the sun emerging after a week of rain.　His father's praise had made him the happiest boy in the world.　As we watched this scene, it reminded us of the power of praise.　And sadly, of how little most of us receive as adults.

37

　　We thought of a story our friend Marty told us.　Marty is a management consultant. He was hired by an Internet company that was just starting its business.　People were too busy and (1)their tempers were reaching the boiling point.　There were a lot of disputes among them.　Toni, a brilliant young woman and a key member of the technical staff, had been working fourteen hours a day, seven days a week.　She said to Marty that a number of job offers were coming her way, and she was tempted to take one. Marty took her aside and asked if there was anything he could do to keep her at the company.

　　"I think you've been doing a great job, but I also have noticed that your stress level is approaching Mt. Everest.　What can I do to help?"　Before she could answer, Toni broke down into tears.　When she pulled herself together, Marty discovered that in addition to the stress of the long hours and the pressure, she hadn't received one word of approval, let alone praise, of her work.　Marty immediately went to Toni's boss and told him (2)the situation.

　　"And while you're at it," he concluded, "a few words of praise for the rest of the staff could only help."

38

　　The boss acted immediately on Marty's suggestion.　An hour after talking to Toni alone in his office, he called all the employees into the conference room.　There on the table was a display of sweets and coffee.　(3)He then proceeded to tell each person how much he appreciated what they had accomplished.　From then on he made it a point to praise an employee when a job was well done.

39

　　"It was a different place after that," Marty told us.　"The boss learned (4)a valuable lesson which he's never forgotten.　And, by the way, Toni became a vice-president and is still with the company.　She's really happy she didn't take another offer."

1

....

2

....

3

....

4

5

....

6

....

語句　　音声は、英語に続いて日本語の意味が読まれます。　　　　　　　　　　CD 1 - Tr 40 〜 43

入試基本レベル

2　**approach** [əpróutʃ]（動）

2　**approach a task**

3　**gather** [gǽðər]（動）

4　**effort** [éfərt]

11　**praise** [préiz]（名）

11　**scene** [síːn]

12　**remind A of B**

15　**hire** [háiər]（動）

22　**notice** [nóutəs]（動）

24　**in addition to ~**

26　**immediately** [imíːdiətli]

28　**conclude** [kənklúːd]

30　**suggestion** [səgdʒéstʃən]

31　**employee** [èmplɔí:]

32　**display** [displéi]

33　**appreciate** [əpríːʃièit]

34　**praise** [préiz]（動）

入試標準レベル（共通テスト・私大）

5　**satisfied** [sǽtisfàid]

10　**emerge** [imə́ːrdʒ]

16　**temper** [témpər]（名）

17　**brilliant** [bríljənt]

24　**break down into tears**

26　**approval** [əprúːvl]

31　**conference** [kánfərəns]

32　**proceed to** *do*

33　**accomplish** [əkámpliʃ]

入試発展レベル（二次・有名私大）

7　**inspect** [inspékt]

17　**dispute** [dispjúːt]（名）

19　**be tempted to** *do*

26　**let alone ~**

33　**make it a point to** *do*

36　**vice-president**

その他

2　**seriousness**　　　　真剣さ

4　**heap** [híːp]（名）　積み重ねたもの、積み重なった山

4　**pat A into B**　　A をたたいて B の形に作る

14　**management consultant**

　　　　　　　　　　　　経営コンサルタント

16　**the boiling point**　沸点、我慢の限界

19　**come** *one's* **way**　（事が）人に起こる

20　**take O aside**　　O を近くに呼ぶ

23　**Mt. Everest**　エベレスト山（比喩的に『頂点、限界』）

24　**pull** *oneself* **together**　冷静になる

28　**while you are at it**　（その）ついでに

30　**act on ~**　　　　　〜に従って行動する

本文解説

1 【with ＋名詞】【現在分詞】

(l.1) He approached his task **with the seriousness** of a construction engineer **working** on a forty-story building.

 ▶ 〈with ＋名詞〉で副詞句を作ることがある。with the seriousness は seriously とほぼ同意。
 e.g. with ease ＝ easily
 ▶ 前置詞 of の目的語は a construction engineer 以下全部で、working は a construction engineer を修飾する現在分詞。「40 階建てのビルに取り組む建築技師」

2 【so ～ that ...】【which : 関係代名詞の非制限用法】

(l.3) He worked **so** hard gathering sand **that** after a half hour he had a large heap of it, **which** he then with great effort patted into a low building.

 ▶ so ～ that ...は「とても～なので…」で、ここでは「一生懸命～したので、30 分後には…だった」。
 ▶ 目的格の関係代名詞 which の先行詞は直前の a large heap of it(= sand)「大きな砂山」。
 ▶ which 以下は and he then with great effort patted it(= a large heap of sand) into a low building と書き換えられる。pat A into B の A の部分に先行詞の内容が入る。

3 【文構造】【無生物主語】【remind A of B】【省略】【前置詞 as】

(l.11) As we watched this scene, it **reminded** us **of** the power of praise. And sadly, **of** how little most of us receive **as** adults.

 ▶ 文の主語 it は this scene を指す無生物主語の文。remind の目的語が us で、直訳では「それ（＝この光景）は私たちに～を思い起こさせた［気づかせた］」となるが、「それを見て～を思い出した［気づいた］」とするとわかりやすい。
 ▶ remind A of B の B は、the power of praise と直後の文の how little ... as adults の 2 つ。
 ▶ how little (praise) most of us receive と、little の後に praise「褒めること」が省略されている。
 ▶ 前置詞 as はここでは「時」を表すと解釈して、「大人になると、大人だと」。

4 【文構造】【話法】【代名詞 one】

(l.18) (S)**She** (V)**said** to Marty (O1)**that a number of job offers were coming her way**, and (O2)**she was tempted to take one**.

 ▶ 全体の構造は She said to Marty that ..., and (that) ... で、2 番目の that が省略されている。
 ▶ トニの発言を直接話法で表すと "A number of job offers are coming my way. I'm tempted to take one (of them)." となる。one は可算名詞を指す代名詞で、ここでは「（そのうちの）1 つ」。

5 【文構造】【let alone】

(l.24) When she pulled herself together, / (S)**Marty** (V)**discovered** (O)**that / in addition to the stress of the long hours and the pressure, / she hadn't received one word of approval, / let alone praise, / of her work**.

 ▶ 全体の構造は When she ..., Marty discovered that (in addition to ～ ,) she hadn't received—「彼女が…すると、マーティは、（～に加えて、）彼女が—をもらっていなかったということがわかった」。
 ▶ let alone ～「～は言うまでもなく」が挿入されて、of her work は approval と praise の 2 つを修飾している。

　各段落のまとめとなるように、空所に適切な語句を入れなさい。（同じ番号には、同じ語句が入ります）

展開	段落	要旨
浜辺の様子①	1	私たちは、少年が浜辺で砂の（①　　　　　）を作るのを見ていた。
浜辺の様子②	2	父親は少年が作った砂山を見て、「すごい（①　　　　　）を作ったね」と言った。
浜辺の様子③	3	父親に褒められた少年の（②　　　　　）を見て、私たちは「（③　　　　　）ことの力」に気づかされた。
友人がしてくれたある会社の話①	4	友人の経営コンサルタントがしてくれたある会社の話を思い出した。その会社の人たちは、あまりにも忙しく、我慢が限界に達していた。ある優秀な女性社員は転職を考えていた。彼は「スタッフへの褒め言葉は役立つだろう」と、彼女の（④　　　　　）に伝えた。
友人がしてくれたある会社の話②	5	その（④　　　　　）は彼の進言に従って、仕事がうまくいったときには必ず従業員を（③　　　　　）ことにした。
友人がしてくれたある会社の話③	6	（④　　　　　）が教訓を学んだことで、会社の状況は改善した。

　「段落要旨」を参考にして、本文全体の内容を百字程度の日本語で要約しなさい。

■　以下を参考にして、「段落要旨」の下線部分を中心にまとめてみよう。
▶「第3、4段落」の内容（70〜80字）
▶「第5、6段落」の内容（20〜30字）

（下書き）

10　　　　　　　　　　20

10　　　　　　　　　　20

In the early 1980s, (1)the Coca-Cola Company ("Coke") was nervous about its 🔊44 future. Once, it had been the (a)dominant soft drink in the world. But Pepsi had been slowly catching up to Coke. In 1972, 18 percent of soft drink users said they drank only Coke, compared with 4 percent who called themselves exclusive Pepsi drinkers.
5 By the early 1980s, Coke had dropped to 12 percent, and Pepsi had risen to 11 percent, despite the fact that Coke was much more widely available than Pepsi and spending at least $100,000,000 more on advertising per year.

Pepsi began running (2)television commercials around the country going head-to- 🔊45 head★ with Coke in what they called the Pepsi Challenge. Dedicated Coke drinkers
10 were asked to take a sip from two glasses, one marked Q and one marked M. Which did they prefer? Almost always, they would say M, and then M would be revealed as Pepsi. When Coke privately did head-to-head blind taste tests of their own, they found the same thing: when asked to choose between Coke and Pepsi, the majority, 57 percent, preferred Pepsi. This news was (b)devastating to Coca-Cola management.

15 Coke's scientists went back and changed the secret formula to make it a little lighter 🔊46 and sweeter — more like Pepsi. Immediately Coke's market researchers noticed an improvement. They tested hundreds of thousands of consumers all across North America, and in head-to-head blind taste tests, New Coke beat Pepsi by 6 to 8 percentage points. Coca-Cola executives were (c)elated. The new drink was given the green
20 light★.

However, it was a disaster. Coke drinkers rose up in outrage against New Coke. 🔊47 There were protests around the country. Coke was in a crisis, and just a few months later, the company was forced to bring back the original formula as Classic Coke. The (3)predicted success of New Coke never happened. But there was an even bigger
25 surprise. (4)For the last twenty years, Coke has competed with Pepsi, with a product that taste tests say is inferior, and it is still the number one soft drink in the world. The story of New Coke, in other words, is a really good example of how complicated it is to find out what people really think.

★ head-to-head「一対一の」 ★ green light「ゴーサイン」

❶

❷

....

....

....

❸ (a) .... (b) .... (c) ....

❹

....

❺

....

....

❻

....

| 語句 | 音声は、英語に続いて日本語の意味が読まれます。 | CD 1 - Tr 48 〜 51 |

入試基本レベル

1 **nervous** [nə́:*r*vəs]

4 **compared with** 〜

6 **despite** [dispáit]

6 **available** [əvéiləbl]

6 **spend A on B**

6 **at least**

11 **prefer** [prifə́:*r*]

12 **taste** [téist]（名）

13 **majority** [mədʒɔ́(:)rəti]

16 **immediately** [imí:diətli]

18 **beat** [bí:t]（動）

21 **disaster** [dizǽstər]

25 **compete with** 〜

入試標準レベル（共通テスト・私大）

2 **dominant** [dámənənt]

3 **catch up to** 〜

4 **call A B**

5 **drop to** 〜

7 **advertising** [ǽdvərtàiziŋ]

8 **commercial** [kəmə́:*r*ʃəl]

9 **what they called** 〜

10 **mark** [má:rk]（動）

11 **reveal A as B**

12 **privately** [práivitli]

12 **blind** [bláind]（形）

13 **choose between** 〜

14 **management** [mǽnidʒmənt]

17 **hundreds of thousands of** 〜

17 **consumer** [kənsú:mər]（名）

19 **executive** [igzékjətiv]（名）

21 **rise up**

22 **protest** [próutest]（名）

22 **crisis** [kráisis]

23 **be forced to** *do*

23 **bring back** 〜

23 **classic** [klǽsik]（形）

24 **predict** [pridíkt]

26 **inferior** [infíəriər]

27 **complicated** [kámpləkèitəd]

入試発展レベル（二次・有名私大）

4 **exclusive** [iksklú:siv]

7 **per** 〜

9 **dedicated** [dédikèitid]

14 **devastating** [dévəstèitiŋ]

15 **formula** [fɔ́:rmjələ]

その他

8 **go head-to-head** 　直接対決する

10 **take a sip** 　一口飲む

18 **percentage point**
　〔率の変化を表す表現〕パーセントポイント

19 **elate** [iléit] 　〜を元気づける

19 **give a green light to** 〜 　〜を許可する

21 **outrage** [áutrèidʒ]（名）　激怒

本文解説

1　【同格の that】【文構造】【spend A on B】

(l.5)　By the early 1980s, Coke had dropped to 12 percent, and Pepsi had risen to 11 percent, despite the fact **that** (S')**Coke** (V'1)**was** much more widely available than Pepsi and (V'2)**spending** at least $100,000,000 more **on** advertising per year.

- ▶ despite は前置詞で、「～にもかかわらず」。despite the fact that Coke was ... は接続詞の although[though] を使って、although[though] Coke was ... と書き換えできる。
- ▶ the fact that Coke was ... の that 以下は the fact の内容を説明する同格表現で、「(that 以下) という現実」の意味。
- ▶ that 節内の述語動詞は、was と (was) spending の 2 つ。
- ▶ spend A on B で「A を B に使う」。A は at least $100,000,000 more だが、more の後に than Pepsi が省略されていて、「ペプシよりも、少なくとも 1 億ドル多く使っていた」ということ。

2　【現在分詞の形容詞的用法】【関係代名詞 what】

(l.8)　Pepsi began running television commercials around the country **going** head-to-head with Coke in **what they called** the Pepsi Challenge.

- ▶ going head-to-head ... は commercials を修飾する現在分詞の形容詞的用法。「コークと直接対決するコマーシャル」
- ▶ what は関係代名詞。what they called the Pepsi Challenge は「彼らがペプシチャレンジと呼んだもの」。what we[they] call ～または what is called ～は「いわゆる」と訳されることが多い定型表現。

3　【by の意味】【percentage point】

(l.17)　They tested hundreds of thousands of consumers all across North America, and in head-to-head blind taste tests, New Coke beat Pepsi **by** 6 to 8 **percentage points**.

- ▶ 前置詞 by は「～の差で」。「6 から 8 (パーセント) ポイントの差でペプシを破った」
- ▶ percentage point「パーセントポイント」は主に「率の変化」を表すときに使う用語。「パーセント」を略して単に「ポイント」と訳されることが多い。たとえば「ペプシ 46%」と「新しいコーク 54%」では New Coke beat Pepsi by 8 percentage points である。

4　【名詞節を導く how】【形式主語】【関係代名詞 what】

(l.26)　The story of New Coke, in other words, is a really good example of **how** complicated **it** is to find out **what** people really think.

- ▶ how complicated it is to find out ...「～を理解することはいかに (複雑で) 困難か (ということ)」の名詞節全体が of の目的語になっている。
- ▶ it は形式主語で、真主語は to find out 以下。how 以下は、It is very complicated to find out ...「…を理解することはとても困難だ」を感嘆文の語順〈How ＋形容詞＋ S V〉にしたもの。
- ▶ find out の目的語は、関係代名詞節の what people really think「人々が実際に考えていること (を理解する)」。間接疑問と解釈して、「人々が実際に何を考えているのか (を理解する)」としても意味は変わらない。

展開	段落	要旨
導入	1	1980 年代初期、コカ・コーラ社は未来に不安を感じていた。それまで支配的な地位にあった（①　　　　　　）が（②　　　　　　　）に追いつかれつつあったからだ。
展開①	2	（①　　　　　　　）は試飲テストで（②　　　　　　　）に敗れた。
展開②	3	（①　　　　　　）は、味をより（②　　　　　　）に近づけるために（③　　　　　　）を変更した。
展開③	4	事前テストで勝利したはずの新しい（①　　　　　　）に消費者は怒り、（①　　　　　　）は元の（③　　　　　　）に戻させざるをえなかった。しかし驚くことに、試飲テストの結果で劣っている製品が、今も世界第 1 位の清涼飲料なのだ。人々が実際に考えていることを理解するのはとても困難なことだ。

■　以下を参考にして、「段落要旨」の下線部分を中心にまとめてみよう。
▶「展開①、②」の内容（25 〜 35 字）
▶「展開③」の内容（70 〜 80 字）
▶字数に余裕があれば、「導入」の内容を適宜追加してもよい。

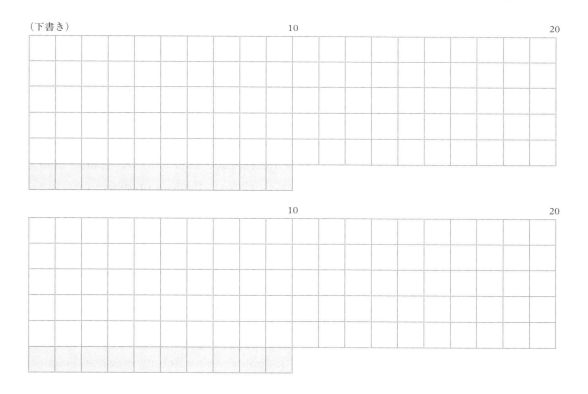

（下書き）　　　　　　　　　　　　　　　　　　10　　　　　　　　　　　　　　　　　　20

CD 1
52

For many humans, social distancing feels like the most unnatural thing in the
world, but in other parts of the natural world, it's the norm. When an infected animal
gets too close, other animals have learned to stay away. To see if animals behaved
differently around infected animals in order to protect themselves from getting sick,
researchers have been conducting studies over the past couple decades.

53

Joseph Kiesecker, lead scientist at The Nature Conservancy's* conservation lands
team, worked on one of the earlier studies and found that American bullfrog tadpoles*
were excellent at social distancing. "It was clear they were showing behavior that
when given the choice to be near an infected individual, they avoided that infected
individual," he said.

54

Kiesecker placed a tadpole infected with a pathogen* around other healthy
tadpoles. The tadpoles could smell the chemicals from the sick tadpole. Detecting it
was infected, the healthy ones stayed away, according to Kiesecker's findings.

55

During part of the study, Kiesecker also tested keeping a healthy tadpole near an
infected one. "When we forced them to stay in close proximity and then observed
whether they were infected or not, the probability that they would get infected increased
based on the proximity that they were to the infected individual," Kiesecker said.

56

Tadpoles aren't the only animals to physically distance themselves from sick
members of their own species. Garden ants also practice social-distancing behaviors
when an infected ant is introduced to a group of healthy ants. Nathalie Stroeymeyt,
a lecturer at the University of Bristol's School of Biological Sciences, observed when
ants with a fungal disease* were introduced to a colony of healthy ants.

57

After observing the colonies once the infected ants were introduced, Stroeymeyt
found that unexposed ants stayed away from the exposed ants and the healthy ants
stayed further away from each other as well. "We believe (1)this is a proactive measure
to decrease the risk of epidemic transmission through the colony, not unlike the form
of proactive social distancing implemented in our societies to decrease the risk of
transmission of Covid-19," Stroeymeyt said.

58

The lessons learned from these animals aren't exclusive to their own species.
Epidemiologists* use studies like these, Kiesecker said, to have a better understanding
of how diseases spread amongst other species — including humans. (2)This allows
people to "alter and change their behavior" to decrease the chance of infection, he said.

59

"Behavior is important," Kiesecker said. "Tadpoles can't watch the news and can't
read news articles that tell them this. People can."

* The Nature Conservancy「1951 年に設立された世界的な自然保護団体（非営利団体）のひとつ」
bullfrog tadpole「ウシガエルのオタマジャクシ」　pathogen「病原体」　fungal disease「真菌性疾患」
epidemiologist「疫学者」

❶ Paragraph 3

experiment：..

result：..

Paragraph 4

experiment：..

result：..

❷ ....

....

❸ ....

....

....

❹ (1) .... (2) ....

| 語句 | 音声は、「英語」→「日本語の意味」の順で読まれます。 | CD 1 - Tr 60 〜 63 |

入試基本レベル

3	learn to *do*	
3	see if 〜	
4	protect O from *doing*	
9	individual [ìndəvídʒuəl]	
9	avoid [əvɔ́id]	
15	force O to *do*	
17	based on 〜	
19	species [spíːʃi(ː)z]	
31	allow O to *do*	
32	chance [tʃǽns]	
33	behavior [bihéivjər]	

入試標準レベル（共通テスト・私大）

2	infected [inféktəd]	
3	stay away	
5	conduct [kəndʌ́kt]（動）	
5	decade [dékèid]	
6	lead [líːd]（形）	
6	conservation [kànsərvéiʃən]	
12	chemical [kémikəl]	
12	detect [ditékt]	

15	observe [əbzə́ːrv]	
16	probability [prɑ̀bəbíləti]	
18	physically [fízikəli]	
18	distance ... from 〜	
22	colony [kɑ́ləni]	
24	unexposed [ʌ̀nikspóuzd]	
24	exposed [ikspóuzd]	
26	transmission [trænsmíʃən]	
32	alter [ɔ́ːltər]	

入試発展レベル（二次・有名私大）

1	unnatural [ʌnnǽtʃərəl]	
2	norm [nɔ́ːrm]	
27	implement [ímpləmènt]（動）	
29	exclusive to 〜	
31	amongst [əmʌ́ŋkst]	

その他

1	social distancing	社会的距離をとること
15	proximity [prɑksíməti]	近さ、近接
25	proactive [prouǽktiv]	事前の策を講じた、予防の
26	epidemic [èpidémik]	伝染病（の）、流行（性の）
28	Covid-19	新型コロナウイルス感染症

本文解説

1 【文構造】【see if ...】【〈目的〉を表す不定詞】【現在完了進行形】

(l.3) **To see if** animals behaved differently around infected animals **in order to protect** themselves from getting sick, researchers **have been conducting** studies over the past couple decades.

▶ 全体の構造は、To see ..., researchers have been conducting studies「…を確かめるために、研究者たちは研究を続けている」。have[has] been *doing* は現在完了進行形で、「（ずっと）〜している、〜してきた」。

▶ see if ... は if 節が see の目的語になっていて、「…かどうかを確かめる」。see whether ... も同意。
   ex. I tasted the leftover a bit to see if it was still good.
   「その残り物がまだ食べられるか、ちょっとだけ試しに食べてみた」

▶ in order to *do*「〜するために」は、〈目的〉を明確に表す不定詞の副詞的用法。ここでは behaved differently を修飾している。

2 【文構造】【that の用法：that の省略、関係副詞（の代用）の that、指示語の that】【〈主語 + be 動詞〉の省略】

(l.8) It was clear **(that)** they were showing behavior **that when given** the choice to be near an infected individual, they avoided **that** infected individual.

▶ 全体の構造は、It was clear (that) ...「…ということははっきりしていた」。真主語である that 節の接続詞 that が省略されている。

▶ behavior に続く that 節はウシガエルのとる行動の説明。that は関係副詞（あるいはその代用）と考えられる。【native speaker の見解】発話をそのまま引用したせいか、文法が少し紛らわしい。behavior in which 〜と言い換えられる。

▶ that infected individual の that は、「その、あの」を意味する指示形容詞。前出の an infected individual を受けて、「その感染した個体」。

▶ when given the choice は、when they were given the choice の意味。副詞節中の主語が主節の主語と一致している場合、〈主語 + be 動詞〉は省略されることが多い。

3 【文構造】【that の用法：同格の that、関係副詞（の代用）の that】

(l.15) When we forced them to stay in close proximity and then observed whether they were infected or not, the probability **that** they would get infected increased based on the proximity **that** they were to the infected individual.

▶ 全体の構造は、When we ..., the probability increased「私たちが…したとき、確率［可能性］は増加した」。

▶ the probability that ... で「…という確率、可能性」。接続詞 that は the probability を説明する〈同格〉節を導いて、その内容を説明している。

▶ the proximity that they were to the infected individual の that は、the proximity を先行詞とする関係副詞（あるいはその代用）。the proximity that S *be* to ... で「S の…までの近接［近さ］」。be in (close) proximity to 〜で「〜に近い」を表すので、the proximity in which they were to the infected individual とも表現できる。
   ex. My school was in close proximity to the harbor.「私の学校は港のすぐ近くにあった」

4 【文構造】【not unlike ...】【過去分詞の後置修飾】

(l.25) We believe this is a proactive measure to decrease the risk of epidemic transmission through the colony, **not unlike** the form of proactive social distancing **implemented** in our societies to decrease the risk of transmission of Covid-19.

▶ 全体の構造は We believe (that) ...「私たちは…だと考えている」で、接続詞 that が省略されている。(that) 節内は、this is a proactive measure ..., not unlike ...「これは…予防策で、…と似ていなくもない」。

▶ not unlike 〜は「〜と似ていないことはない、〜と大して違わない、〜と五十歩百歩だ（≒ similar to 〜）」の意味を表す。

▶ implemented 以下は、the form of proactive social distancing「予防的な社会的距離をとる形」を修飾する過去分詞句。

展開	段落	要旨
序論	1	人間には（①　　　　　　　　　　　　　）をとることは不自然に感じられるが、動物界では普通のことだ。動物が、感染した仲間がいると感染防止の行動をとるのか、長年研究が行われている。
本論①	2	ザ・ネイチャー・コンサーバンシーのキーゼッカー氏は、ウシガエルのオタマジャクシが感染を避ける行動をとることを発見した。
本論②	3	オタマジャクシは、病原体に感染したオタマジャクシが出す化学物質の（②　　　　　　）から仲間の感染を感知して、距離をとった。
本論③	4	感染したオタマジャクシと健康なオタマジャクシを強制的に一緒にしておくと、感染した個体との（③　　　　）に応じて感染の（④　　　　　　）が高まった。
本論④	5	オタマジャクシだけが社会的距離をとる唯一の動物ではない。ストロイメイト氏は、庭アリが同様の行動をとるかを観察した。
本論⑤	6	感染したアリをコロニーに入れると、感染したアリと健康なアリだけでなく健康なアリ同士も距離をとる、（⑤　　　　　　　）と思われる行動をとった。
結論①	7	動物の行動の研究を通して、（⑥　　　）を含む他の種の病気の拡散についても理解が深まる。
結論②	8	情報のない動物たちが感染（⑤　　　　　　）をとれるのだから、それは（⑥　　　　　　）にもできるはずだ。

百字要約　　「段落要旨」を参考にして、本文全体の内容を百字程度の日本語で要約しなさい。

■ 以下を参考にして、「段落要旨」の下線部分を中心にまとめてみよう。
　▶「序論」の内容（20〜30字）　　▶「本論」の内容（40〜60字）　　▶「結論」の内容（20〜30字）

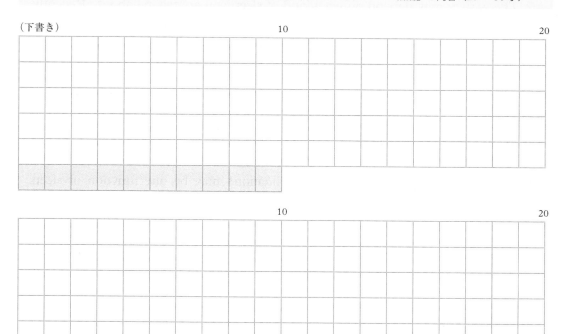

（下書き）

🔊 64

If we don't know why we can't sleep, it's in part because we don't really know why we need to sleep in the first place. We know we miss it if we don't have it. And we know that (1)no matter how much we try to resist it, sleep conquers us in the end. We know that seven to nine hours after giving in to sleep, most of us are ready to get up again, and 15 to 17 hours after that we are tired once more. We have known for 50 years that we divide our slumber★ between periods of deep-wave sleep and what is called rapid eye movement (REM) sleep, when (2)(active / as / as / awake / is / the brain / we're / when), but our voluntary muscles are paralyzed★. We know that all mammals and birds sleep. A dolphin sleeps with half its brain awake so it can remain aware of its underwater environment. When mallard ducks★ sleep in a line, the two outermost birds are able to keep half of their brains alert and one eye open to guard against predators★. Fish, reptiles, and insects all experience some kind of repose too.

🔊 65

All this downtime★ comes (3)at a price. An animal must lie still for a great stretch of time, during which it is easy prey for predators. What can possibly be the payback★ for such risk? "If sleep doesn't serve an absolutely vital function," the renowned sleep researcher Allan Rechtschaffen once said, "it is the greatest mistake evolution ever made."

🔊 66

The predominant theory of sleep is that the brain demands it. This idea derives in part from common sense — whose head doesn't feel clearer after a good night's sleep? But the trick is to confirm this assumption with real data. (4)How does sleeping help the brain? The answer may depend on what kind of sleep you are talking about. Recently, researchers at Harvard led by Robert Stickgold tested undergraduates★ on various aptitude★ tests, allowed them to nap, then tested them again. They found that those who had engaged in REM sleep subsequently performed better in pattern recognition tasks, such as grammar, while those who slept deeply were better at memorization. Other researchers have found that the sleeping brain appears to repeat a pattern of neuron firing that occurred while the subject★ was recently awake, as if in sleep the brain were trying to commit to long-term memory what it had learned that day.

🔊 67

Such studies suggest that memory consolidation★ may be one function of sleep. Giulio Tononi, a noted sleep researcher at the University of Wisconsin, Madison, published an interesting twist★ on this theory a few years ago: His study showed that the sleeping brain seems to weed out redundant or unnecessary synapses★ or connections. So (5)the purpose of sleep may be to help us remember what's important, by letting us forget what's not.

★ slumber「眠り、まどろみ」 paralyze「麻痺させる、しびれさせる」 mallard duck「マガモ」 predator「捕食動物」 downtime「停止時間」 payback「見返り」 undergraduate「学部学生」 aptitude「適性」 subject「被験者」 consolidation「定着」 twist「予想外の進展」 synapse「シナプス（神経細胞の連接部）」

1
....

....

2
....

3
....

....

4
....

....

5
....

....

6
....

語句	音声は、英語に続いて日本語の意味が読まれます。	CD 1 - Tr 68 ～ 71

入試基本レベル

2 **miss** [mís]（動）

9 **remain** [riméin]

11 **guard** [gáːrd]（動）

25 **task** [tǽsk]（名）

29 **suggest** [sʌdʒést]

入試標準レベル（共通テスト・私大）

1 **in part because ～**

2 **in the first place**

3 **resist** [rizíst]

3 **conquer** [káŋkər]

4 **give in to ～**

6 **divide A between B and C**

6 **what is called**

7 **awake** [əwéik]（形）

8 **mammal** [mǽml]

9 **aware of ～**

10 **in a line**（= in line）

13 **lie still**

15 **absolutely** [ǽbsəlùːtli]

15 **vital** [váitl]

16 **evolution** [èvəlúːʃn]

18 **demand** [dimǽnd]（動）

18 **derive from ～**

18 **in part**

19 **common sense**

20 **confirm** [kənfəːrm]

20 **assumption** [əsʌ́mpʃn]

24 **engage in ～**

24 **recognition** [rèkəgníʃn]

28 **commit A to memory** — A を記憶にとどめる

28 **long-term**

入試発展レベル（二次・有名私大）

11 **alert** [əláːrt]（形）

13 **at a price**

13 **a stretch of A**

15 **serve a function**

15 **renowned** [rináund]

18 **predominant** [pridámənənt]

23 **nap** [nǽp]（動）

24 **subsequently** [sʌ́bsəkwntli]

25 **memorization** [mèməraizéiʃən]

30 **noted** [nóutid]

その他

7 **rapid eye movement** — 急速眼球運動

8 **voluntary muscle** — 随意筋

10 **outermost** [áutərmòust]（形） — 最も外側の

12 **reptile** [réptl] — 爬（は）虫類の動物

12 **repose** [ripóuz]（名） — 休息、睡眠

14 **be prey for ～** — ～の餌食になる

20 **The trick is to** *do* — ～するのが大事[こつ]だ

27 **neuron firing** — ニューロン発火

32 **weed out ～** — ～を取り除く

32 **redundant** [ridʌ́ndənt] — 余分な

本文解説

1 【文構造】【関係代名詞 what】【関係副詞 when】【比較 as ... as 〜】

(l.5) We have known for 50 years / that we divide our slumber / between periods of deep-wave sleep and **what** is called rapid eye movement (REM) sleep, **when** (active / as / as / awake / is / the brain / we're / when), but our voluntary muscles are paralyzed.

▶ 全体の構文は We have known ... that 〜「私たちは〜ということを知っている」。that 節内は we divide our slumber between A and B「私たちは眠りを A と B に分けている」。

▶ what is called は関係代名詞 what を用いた慣用表現で「いわゆる」という意味。

▶ when 以下は rapid eye movement(REM) sleep を先行詞とする関係副詞。when は in which と同意で「その睡眠中には」。

▶ 並べ替えの部分は問題の指示文の日本語から as...as 〜が思いつく。比較しているものは「私たちが起きている時」と「睡眠中」の脳の状態。

▶ when 以下は REM sleep の説明。A, but B の B の部分は「随意筋は麻痺している」。

2 【修辞疑問文】

(l.18) This idea derives in part from common sense — **whose head** doesn't feel clearer after a good night's sleep?

▶ This idea は前の文の「脳が睡眠を必要としているから睡眠が必要」という内容を指す。

▶ —（ダッシュ）のあとの疑問文は common sense「常識」の内容。

▶ Whose は「誰の〜」を聞く疑問詞。直訳は「誰の頭が一晩十分に寝た後でよりすっきり感じないだろうか」で、「そんなことはない」という意味の修辞疑問文。したがって、Everyone's head feels clearer after a good night's sleep.「みんなの頭は一晩ぐっすり寝るとよりすっきりする」という意。good は「たっぷり」の意。

3 【文構造】【関係代名詞 that】【as if】【commit A to memory】

(l.26) Other researchers have found / that the sleeping brain appears to repeat a pattern of neuron firing / **that** occurred / while the subject was recently awake, / **as if** in sleep the brain were trying to commit to long-term memory / what it had learned that day.

▶ 全体の構造は Other researchers have found that 〜「他の研究者は〜ということを発見している」の SVO の文。that 節内は the sleeping brain appears to repeat 〜「寝ている脳は〜を繰り返しているように見える」。

▶ 2 番目の that は a pattern of neuron firing「ニューロン発火のパターン」を先行詞とする関係詞節で、「被験者が直前に起きている間に発生した」。

▶ as if 〜の節は repeat を修飾する副詞節で「まるで〜かのようにパターンを繰り返す」と続く。

▶ commit A to (long-term) memory で「A を長期記憶する」。A の部分が what it had learned that day「その日に学習したこと」と長いため、倒置が起きて commit to long-term memory A の語順になっている。

展開	段落	要旨
導入	1	私たちは睡眠について分かっていない。睡眠が（①　　　　　）睡眠と（②　　　　　）睡眠に分けられることや、全ての生物が睡眠やある種の休息をとることは分かっている。
本論①	2	睡眠には、捕食動物の餌食になるという（③　　　　　）が伴う。
本論②	3	（④　　　　　）が睡眠を要求しているという理論が有力だ。睡眠の種類によって適性検査の結果が変化することや、睡眠中の（④　　　　　）が（⑤　　　　　）を定着させているように見えることが発見されている。
結論	4	それらの研究は睡眠が（⑤　　　　　）定着機能を持つことを示唆している。さらに別の研究によれば、睡眠中の（④　　　　　）が不必要なことを忘れさせることで、重要なことを記憶する手助けをしている可能性があるようだ。

■ 以下を参考にして、「段落要旨」の下線部分を中心にまとめてみよう。
  ▶「導入」の内容（15 ～ 20字）
  ▶「本論①、②」の内容（40 ～ 50字）
  ▶「各論③」の内容（35 ～ 45字）

（下書き）

10　　　　　　　　　　　　　　　　　20

10　　　　　　　　　　　　　　　　　20

CD 1
72

"Truth" is probably the greatest barrier to good communication. During an argument with a friend or your spouse★, you may have such a powerful conviction that you are right that you don't try to see the other person's point of view. Instead, you argue and try to force them to agree with you. (1)This never works. You've probably
5 noticed that the more you try to persuade the other person to agree with you, the more argumentative he or she becomes. This is because you're not really listening to their viewpoint. They believe their feelings are being ignored, and they'll argue louder and longer to try to get you to listen. You both end up feeling angry and frustrated.

73

You may be completely unaware you're doing this. A woman's husband recently
10 said, "Sarah, you always do exactly what you want without considering my needs. You put your career and your needs first." Sarah replied, "No, I don't. You are my priority, Harold, but sometimes my studies have to take precedence★ if I have a big exam coming up." Although Sarah might think she's being honest and reasonable, she has made the mistake of suggesting that she's right and he's wrong about this. The moment
15 she contradicts★ him, (2)she proves that he's right. In point of fact, she's not trying to understand his point of view, she's only tuned in★ to her needs and her own view of the situation. That's exactly what he's complaining about!

74

(3) So what's the alternative? She could express her feelings with "I feel" statements. How does she feel? She feels ticked off★! So why not just say this instead
20 of being argumentative? She could also try to understand what he's thinking and feeling. How does he feel? He feels shut out and ignored. She could say, "I feel put down★ and angry, but I know there's some truth in what you say. Apparently you think I've put my career first and you feel rejected. Is this the way you feel? If so, I could understand why you feel hurt and angry."

75

(4) I've worked with hundreds of people with troubled relationships, and
25 practically every one of them has made the same mistake of arguing about the "truth." This strategy never helped anyone resolve a problem. When you feel upset, you will have a tremendous urge to explain why your ideas and feelings are valid★. *Don't do it!* You will have a tremendous urge to defend yourself and argue. *Don't do it!* What
30 usually happens when you try to point out the truth to someone? When you argued and got defensive, did your spouse ever stop arguing and say, "Thank you, thank you for opening my eyes. I see now where I was so wrong"? (A)

76

The key to resolving an argument is often to back off★ and try a different approach. The bottom line is that you must never defend the "truth!" (5)Your "truth" is your
35 enemy! When you give up the idea that you have a monopoly★ on the truth and you try to understand the other person's point of view, you will find that people will be much more willing to listen to you and to understand your own point of view.

★spouse「配偶者」　take precedence「優先する」　contradict「否定する」　tune in「耳を傾ける」　tick off「叱責する」
put down「批判する」　valid「正当な根拠のある」　back off「一歩引く」　monopoly「独占権」

1
....

2
....

....

3 (i) .... (ii) ....

4 ....

5
....

....

| 語句 | 音声は、英語に続いて日本語の意味が読まれます。 | CD 1 - Tr 77 〜 80 |

入試基本レベル

2	**argument** [ɑ́:rgjəmənt]	
4	**argue** [ɑ́:rgju:]	
4	**force A to** *do*	
7	**loud** [láud] （副）	
8	**end up (by)** *doing*	
12	**exam** [igzǽm]	
13	**honest** [ɑ́(:)nəst]	
13	**reasonable** [rí:zənəbl]	
14	**suggest** [səgdʒést]	
15	**prove** [prú:v]	
17	**complain about** 〜	
19	**statement** [stéitmənt]	
22	**apparently** [əpǽrəntli]	
23	**reject** [ridʒékt] （動）	
27	**upset** [ʌpsét] （動）	
35	**enemy** [énəmi] （名）	

入試標準レベル（共通テスト・私大）

1	**barrier** [bǽriər] （名）	
5	**persuade A to** *do*	
7	**ignore** [ignɔ́:r]	
8	**frustrated** [frʌ́streitid]	
11	**career** [kəríər] （名）	
11	**priority** [praiɔ́(:)rəti]	
16	**tune in (to** 〜 **)**	（〜に）耳を傾ける
18	**alternative** [ɔ:ltə́:rnətiv] （名）	
21	**shut out** 〜	
26	**practically** [prǽktikəli]	

27	**strategy** [strǽtədʒi]	
27	**resolve** [rizá(:)lv] （動）	
28	**tremendous** [trəméndəs]	
28	**urge** [ə́:rdʒ] （名）	
29	**defend** [difénd]	
30	**point out** 〜	
31	**defensive** [difénsiv]	
36	**be willing to** *do*	

入試発展レベル （二次・有名私大）

2	**spouse** [spáus]	配偶者
7	**viewpoint** [vjú:pɔ̀int]	
9	**unaware** [ʌnəwéər]	
12	**take precedence**	優先する
15	**contradict** [kɑ̀ntrədíkt]	否定する、反論する
15	**in point of fact**	
21	**put down**	批判する
25	**troubled** [trʌ́bld]	
28	**valid** [vǽlid]	正当な根拠のある
35	**monopoly** [mənápəli]	独占権

その他

2	**conviction** [kənvíkʃən]	確信
6	**argumentative** [à:rgjəméntətiv]	議論好きの、理屈っぽい
11	**put A first**	A を第一に考える
19	**tick off** 〜	〜を叱責する
33	**back off**	一歩引く
34	**The bottom line is that ...**	要するに…だ

本文解説

1　【such ～ that ...】【同格の that】

(l.1)　During an argument with a friend or your spouse, you may have **such** a powerful conviction **that** you are right **that** you don't try to see the other person's point of view.

- ▶ 全体の構文は、During ～ , you may have such ... conviction ... that you don't try to － .「～の間、…という確信があるので、－しようとしないかもしれない」。
- ▶ conviction に続く that は、名詞 conviction「確信」の具体的な内容を説明する「同格の that」。that の前には idea、doubt、belief、hope、desire、news、possibility など、具体的内容を必要とする名詞がくる。
- ▶ you are right に続く that は、such と相関をなす、such ～ that ...「非常に～なので、…だ」の that。

2　【the ＋比較級 ..., the ＋比較級 ～】【persuade A to do】

(l.4)　You've probably noticed that **the more** you try to **persuade** the other person **to agree** with you, **the more** argumentative he or she becomes.

- ▶ the more you try to ..., the more argumentative he or she becomes ～ の部分は、you try more to ... ＋ he or she becomes more argumentative がもとになる形。「…しようとすればするほど、その人はますます～になる」の意味になる。
- ▶ persuade A to do「A を説得して～させる」

3　【状態動詞の進行形】【前置詞 of：同格】

(l.13)　Although Sarah might think she**'s being** honest and reasonable, she has made the mistake **of** suggesting that she's right and he's wrong about this.

- ▶ she's being honest は「彼女は正直であろうとしている」。be 動詞は状態動詞で通例進行形は作らないが、「（一時的・あるいは意識的に）～している」という意味では進行形になる。
  - *cf.* He is being very kind to my son.「彼は私の息子にとても親切にしてくれています」
- ▶ 前置詞句 of suggesting that ... は、先行する名詞 mistake の内容を説明する同格表現。「…ということを示唆するという誤り」
- ▶ he's wrong about this の前に、接続詞 that が省略されている。前の that she's right とともに、suggesting の目的語になっている。

4　【同格の that】【be willing to do】

(l.35)　When you give up the idea **that** you have a monopoly on the truth and you try to understand the other person's point of view, you will find that people will **be** much more **willing to listen** to you and to understand your own point of view.

- ▶ 全体の構文は、When you give up the idea ～ and you try to understand ..., you will find that － .「あなたが～という考えをやめて、…を理解しようとするとき、－だとわかるだろう」。
- ▶ 接続詞 that は、idea の内容を説明する同格の that。「～という考え」
- ▶ people will be much more willing to ...「人々ははるかに快く…してくれるだろう」 be willing to do は「～する意志［気］がある、～してもかまわない」の意。

展開	段落	要旨
導入	1	自分が「（① 　　　　　　　）」だと考えていることを主張し、相手をそれに同意させようとすると、（② 　　　　　　　　　　）はうまくいかない。
本論①	2	あなたは、自分が相手に「（① 　　　　　　　）」を押しつけて、相手の視点を無視していることに全く気づいていないかもしれない。
本論②	3	問題の解決策は、自分の（③ 　　　　　　　　）を正直に語ると同時に、相手の立場を尊重することだ。
本論③	4	（④ 　　　　　　　　）のトラブルを抱えているほぼ全員が、「（① 　　　　　　）」について言い争うという間違いを犯している。
結論	5	「（① 　　　　　　　）」を捨て、相手の視点を理解しようとすれば、相手もこちらの視点を理解するようになるだろう。「（① 　　　　　　）」とはあなたの（⑤ 　　　　）なのである。

■　以下を参考にして、「段落要旨」の下線部分を中心にまとめてみよう。
▶「導入」の内容（40〜50字）
▶「本論①」の内容（15〜25字）
▶「結論」の内容（40〜50字）

（下書き）

"Organic": in less than a century, the term has become a symbol of quality and tradition. Nowadays, we are offered a wealth of organic products never imagined by organic pioneers. In recent years, products have appeared in shopping areas and superstores claiming to be "100% organic," or to contain "no artificial additives★." From salads to skincare products, shoppers have an incredible range to choose from.

But how much better are those products than non-organic products? Do they really help protect the environment? Are they better for your health? (1)The one thing you can be sure about is that they'll probably cost twice as much! So how can you know what you're getting and whether it's worth it?

The largest sector of organic products is still food, both as separate products and as ingredients in everything from breakfast cereals to ice-cream. Supporters claim that these products taste better and are better for you. Critics say there is no nutritional difference.

In recent years, public demand for these products has increased enormously, driven by scares over the possible health risks of chemical pesticides. However, the debate continues over whether or not these risks really exist. (2)Both sides present evidence from scientific studies. First, consumers are told that pesticides can cause cancer, especially in children. Then, other equally qualified scientists say the fears are exaggerated. So, who can you trust?

Despite denials by many scientists and large agribusinesses, (3)there seems reason to be cautious. Recently, a study that tested 957 non-organic foods found that 203 still had some pesticides, including nearly all of the bread tested. While the study claimed that the amounts found were safe, other scientists say our understanding of the effects of pesticides on human health is still very limited.

We don't really know the amount of pesticides we can safely consume. So it is probably a good idea to consume less of them. But can you afford to? Not everyone can pay the high prices necessary to buy organic food regularly. While organic eggs, for example, may cost only 50 percent more than the regular kind, an organic chicken can sometimes cost six times the price of a factory-farmed one.

It's easy to forget that without industrial farming methods, we simply wouldn't have so much cheap food. Are we prepared to give up meat every day and return to having it less frequently like our grandparents did?

Of course, many people say we should. They provide not only health reasons but ethical and ecological ones, too. They argue that we have quickly gone from (4)(food, having, having, little, much, to, too, too), and that we have become used to a way of life that is destroying our environment and harming our health. Their critics, on the other hand, say $_{(5)}$it's too idealistic to think we can produce the food the world needs organically.

9　　The main problem with organics seems to be that although it opposes big business, it is also becoming big business. You may feel that the organic Indonesian oils in your shampoo do wonders for your hair. But shipping shampoo halfway across the world　40 certainly isn't going to help stop the greenhouse effect. And does the supermarket selling it to you really care about the conditions of the workers who produce it? Many organic products are unsustainable. They may be good for us, but are they good for the planet? Perhaps we should be replacing the word "organic" with "local" and "hand-made." Or, perhaps, we should just do like some of our grandparents did and grow our own food.　45

* additive: a substance that is added to food to improve its taste, appearance etc.

1　..
....

2　...
....

3　..
....

4　...

5　..
....

6　① ....　② ....　③ ....　④ ....　⑤ ....

| 語句 | 音声は、英語に続いて日本語の意味が読まれます。 | CD 2 - Tr 10 ～ 13 |

入試基本レベル

1　**quality** [kwάləti]（名）_____

5　**range** [réindʒ]（名）_____

5　**choose from ～** _____

9　**worth** [wə́ːrθ]（形）_____

13　**public** [pʌ́blik]（形）_____

22　**effect** [ifékt]（名）_____

26　**regularly** [régjələrli] _____

27　**regular** [régjələr]（形）_____

30　**be prepared to** _do_ _____

33　**argue** [άːrgjuː] _____

38　**oppose** [əpóuz] _____

42　**care about ～** _____

入試標準レベル（共通テスト・私大）

1　**term** [tə́ːrm]（名）_____

2　**a wealth of ～** _____

4　**artificial** [ὰːrtifíʃəl] _____

5　**incredible** [inkrédəbl] _____

13　**demand** [dimǽnd]（名）_____

13　**enormously** [inɔ́ːrməsli] _____

14　**scare** [skéər]（名）_____

14　**chemical** [kémikəl]（形）_____

15　**evidence** [évid(ə)ns]（名）_____

16　**consumer** [kənsúːmər]（名）_____

_____

17　**equally** [íːkwəli] _____

17　**exaggerate** [igzǽdʒərèit] _____

20　**cautious** [kɔ́ːʃəs] _____

23　**limited** [límitid]（形）_____

24　**consume** [kənsúːm] _____

25　**can afford to** _do_ _____

31　**frequently** [fríːkwəntli] _____

33　**ethical** [éθikəl] _____

33　**ecological** [ìːkəládʒikəl] _____

41　**greenhouse effect** _____

44　**replace A with B** _____

入試発展レベル（二次・有名私大）

1　**organic** [ɔːrgǽnik] _____

10　**sector** [séktər] _____

11　**ingredient** [ingríːdiənt] _____

12　**critic** [krítik] _____

12　**nutritional** [nuːtríʃənəl] _____

13　**drive** [dráiv]（動）_____

14　**pesticide** [péstəsàid] _____

17　**qualified** [kwάləfàid]（形）

_____

19　**denial** [dináiəl] _____

36　**idealistic** [aidìːəlístik]（形）_____

40　**ship** [ʃíp]（動）_____

その他

5　**skincare** 　　肌の手入れ（用）の

19　**agribusiness** 　　農業関連企業

28　**factory-farmed** 　　工場畜産された

29　**industrial farming** 　　工業化された農業

40　**do wonders for ～** 　　～に驚くほど効果がある

43　**unsustainable** [ʌ̀nsəstéinəbl]

　　持続可能でない

1 【文構造】【claim の用法】

(l.3) In recent years, (S)<u>products</u> (V)<u>have appeared</u> in shopping areas and superstores (C)<u>claiming</u> to be "100% organic," or to contain "no artificial additives."

- ▶ 文の基本構造は、products have appeared claiming ... 。直訳は「製品が…と主張して現れている」あるいは「製品が現れ、〜と主張している」だが、claiming 以下を主語 products を説明する現在分詞句と解釈して、「〜と主張する製品が現れている」としてもかまわない。
- ▶ claim は「主張する」が基本的な意味だが、通例、主張内容の真偽が定かでないことを意味する。英英辞典も "to state that something is true, even though it has not been proved" と定義している。日本語にも「"無添加" とうたった製品」や「"デジタル対応テレビ" と銘打った製品」などという表現があるが、この文も「"100% オーガニック" や "人工添加物なし" をうたう製品が現れている」といった意味である。
- ▶ claim の目的語となる不定詞句は、to be "100% organic" と to contain "no artificial additives" の2つ。

2 【文構造】【相関語句：both as A and as B, everything from A to B】

(l.10) (S)<u>The largest sector</u> of organic products (V)<u>is</u> still (C)<u>food</u>, **both as** separate products **and as** ingredients in **everything from** breakfast cereals **to** ice-cream.

- ▶ 文の基本構造は、The largest sector is food.「最大の分野は食品である」。
- ▶ both 以下は、前半で言及されているオーガニック食品の補足説明をしている。both as A and as B「A としても、また B としても」の形になっていて、A は separate products「個別の商品」、B は ingredients ...「…の材料」である。
- ▶ everything from A to B で「A から B までのありとあらゆるもの」。from A to B は数値、場所、種類、分野などの範囲を表すときに便利な表現である。

3 【文構造】【while〈対比〉】【動名詞句】

(l.21) **While** the study claimed that the amounts found were safe, other scientists say **our understanding of the effects of pesticides on human health** is still very limited.

- ▶ While ... safe までが従属節、other scientists 以下が主節。while は〈対比〉の意味を表して、「…の一方で」。ここでは、農薬の残存量の安全性に対する2つの見解を対比して提示している。
- ▶ the amounts found の found は、the amounts を後置修飾している過去分詞。the amounts which were found「(食品中に) 見つかった (農薬の) 量」の意味。
- ▶ 主節の say 以下、(that が省略された) 名詞節の主部である動名詞句 our understanding of the effects of ... は、"we understand the effects of ..." の名詞表現と考えるとよい。「私たちが…の影響を理解すること」、つまり「…の影響についての私たちの理解」という意味。effect of A on B で「A の B への影響」。主部全体で「農薬の人の健康への影響についての私たちの理解」。

4 【仮定法：without 〜】【simply ... not】

(l.29) It's easy to forget that **without** industrial farming methods, we **simply wouldn't have** so much cheap food.

- ▶ it is easy to forget that ...「…ということを忘れるのは簡単だ」は、「…ということを忘れがちだ」とするとより自然な日本語となる。
- ▶ that 節中は、without 〜, we wouldn't have ...「〜がなければ、私たちは…を持つことはないだろうに」という仮定法過去の文。without は if を用いない仮定の表現。if it were not for ... あるいは if we didn't have[use] ... とも表現できる。
- ▶ simply ... not の語順で、「とても…ない、全然…でない」。

段落要旨　各段落のまとめとなるように、空所に適切な語句を入れなさい。（同じ番号には、同じ語句が入ります）

展開	段落	要旨
序論	1	「オーガニック」という言葉は（①　　　　）と（②　　　　）の象徴となった。今日、信じられないほど豊富なオーガニック製品が提供されている。
序論②	2	オーガニック製品が非オーガニック製品と比べて、どれほど優れているかはわからない。
本論①	3	オーガニック製品の最大分野は（③　　　　）であるが、その是非については意見が分かれる。
本論②	4	近年、化学農薬に対する（④　　　　）から、オーガニック製品への需要が非常に増加している。だが、農薬が本当に危険かどうかについては論争中である。
本論③	5	科学者や農業関連企業が否定しても、農薬への用心はすべきだろう。（⑤　　　　）の約5分の1に農薬が残っていた、とする研究結果もあるからだ。
本論④	6	安全に摂取できる農薬の量がよくわからないため、その消費量を（⑥　　　　）方が賢明だろう。
本論⑤	7	（⑦　　　　）なしでは、これほど多くの安価な食品を得ることは不可能だろう。
本論⑥	8	多くの人が健康、倫理、生態学的な理由からオーガニック食品に賛成している。一方で、世界中の食料を有機的に生産できると考えるのは（⑧　　　　）すぎると批判する人もいる。
結論	9	オーガニックの主な問題は、それ自身もまた（⑨　　　　）になりつつあることだ。多くのオーガニック製品は持続可能ではなく、地球にとってよいとは言えないだろう。

百字要約　「段落要旨」を参考にして、本文全体の内容を百字程度の日本語で要約しなさい。

（下書き）

									10										20

									10										20

Memo

The spread of driver-assistance technology will be gradual over the next few years. ✎14
However, in the not-too-distant future fully (a)<u>autonomous cars</u> will most likely become
a reality. When they do, they will make (b)<u>existing cars</u> look as old-fashioned as steam
engines★ and landline telephones★.

5 For a vision of this future, visit Heathrow airport outside London, and head to ✎15
a "pod★ parking" area. Transfers between the car park and terminal are provided
by driverless electric pods moving on dedicated roadways above the street. Using a
touchscreen kiosk, you summon a pod and specify your destination. A pod, which
can seat four people, pulls up, parks itself, and opens its doors. Jump in, sit down, and
10 press the start button. It drives you to your destination, avoiding other pods and neatly
parking itself when you arrive, before heading off to pick up its next passengers.

(c)<u>Self-driving cars</u> have enormous benefits. Today 94% of car accidents are due ✎16
to human error, and the three leading causes are alcohol, speeding, and interruptions.
Accidents kill around 1.2 million people a year worldwide. (d)<u>Driverless cars</u> cannot
15 drink alcohol, break the speed limit, or get interrupted by a text message, so accidents
should occur much less often. A new study estimates that (1)<u>if 90% of cars on American
roads were autonomous, the number of accidents would fall from 5.5 million a year to
1.3 million, and road deaths from 32,400 to 11,300.</u>

As well as being safer, self-driving vehicles would make traffic flow more smoothly, ✎17
20 because they would not brake unpredictably, could be routed to avoid crowded roads,
and could travel close together. All of these factors would increase road capacity. A
study by the University of Texas estimates that (2)<u>if 90% of cars in America were self-
driving it would be equivalent to a doubling of road capacity.</u> Delays would be cut by
60% on motorways and 15% on suburban roads. And riders in self-driving vehicles
25 would be able to do other things. The resulting productivity gains would be worth $1.3
trillion a year in America and $5.6 trillion worldwide. Children, the elderly and the
disabled could gain more independence.

(3)<u>With cars in constant use, much less parking space would be needed.</u> Parking ✎18
accounts for as much as 24% of the area of American cities. Some urban areas have
30 as many as 3.5 parking spaces per car; even so, people looking for parking account for
30% of total driving time in urban business districts. By liberating space wasted on
parking, autonomous vehicles could allow more people to live in city centers; but they
would also make it easier for workers to live farther out. If you can sleep on the trip, a
longer commute becomes feasible.

35 Car-lovers will doubtless regret the passing of machines that, in the 20th century, ✎19
became symbols of personal freedom. But in a future without drivers, people will come
to wonder why they tolerated such a high rate of road deaths, and why they spent so
much money on machines that mostly sat unused. A world of self-driving vehicles may
sound odd, but coming generations will probably consider the era of car ownership to

have been much stranger.

   ★   steam engine「蒸気機関車」   landline telephone「固定電話」   pod「ポッド（カプセル状の乗り物）」

❶   ....

❷

❸

❹

❺   (A) ....   (B) ....

| 語句 | 音声は、英語に続いて日本語の意味が読まれます。 | CD 2 - Tr 20 〜 23 |

入試基本レベル

1	**spread** [spréd]（名）	
1	**gradual** [grǽdʒuəl]	
2	**likely** [láikli]（副）	
3	**reality** [ri(:)ǽləti]（名）	現実のもの
6	**provide** [prəváid]	
7	**roadway** [róudwèi]	
12	**due to** 〜	
21	**factor** [fǽktər]	
23	**delay** [diléi]（名）	
29	**as much as** 〜	
30	**as many as** 〜	

入試標準レベル（共通テスト・私大）

2	**fully** [fúli]	
3	**existing** [igzístiŋ]	
5	**vision** [víʒən]	
5	**head** [héd]（動）	
8	**destination** [dèstənéiʃən]	
13	**interruption** [ìntərʌ́pʃən]	
15	**interrupt** [ìntərʌ́pt]（動）	
16	**estimate** [éstəmèit]（動）	
19	**smoothly** [smúːðli]	
19	**vehicle** [víːəkl]	
21	**capacity** [kəpǽsəti]	
23	**equivalent** [ikwívələnt]	
24	**suburban** [səbə́ːrbən]	
25	**productivity** [pròudʌktívəti]	

26	**the disabled**	
27	**independence** [indipéndəns]	
29	**account for** 〜	
29	**urban** [ə́ːrbən]	
31	**district** [dístrikt]	
31	**liberate** [líbərèit]	
35	**regret** [rigrét]	
39	**odd** [ɑ́d]	

入試発展レベル（二次・有名私大）

2	**autonomous** [ɔːtánəməs]	
3	**old-fashioned**	
6	**transfer** [trǽnsfəːr]（名）	
7	**dedicated** [dédikèitid]	
8	**specify** [spésəfài]	
10	**neatly** [níːtli]	
20	**unpredictably** [ʌ̀npridíktəbli]	
20	**route** [rúːt]（動）	
35	**doubtless** [dáutləs]	
37	**tolerate** [tálərèit]	

その他

2	**not-too-distant**	それほど遠くない
8	**summon** [sʌ́mən]	呼び出す
9	**pull up**	止まる
13	**speeding** [spíːdiŋ]	速度違反
23	**doubling** [dʌ́bliŋ]	倍増（すること）
34	**feasible** [fíːzəbl]	実行可能な
35	**passing** [pǽsiŋ]	消滅

11. Part 3

本文解説

1 【as well as ～】【使役動詞 make】【文構造】【仮定法過去】

(l.19) **As well as** being safer, self-driving vehicles **would make traffic flow** more smoothly, because they **would** not brake unpredictably, **could** be routed to avoid crowded roads, and **could** travel close together.

▶ as well as ～は「～ばかりでなく、～に加えて（= in addition to ～）」。前置詞的に使われ、ここでは後に動名詞が続いている。

▶ make は使役動詞の用法で、(S)self-driving vehicles (V)would make (O)traffic (動詞の原形)flow more smoothly「自動運転の乗り物は、交通をもっと円滑に流れるようにするだろう」の意味。「自動運転車によって、交通は今までより円滑に流れるようになるだろう」とすると日本語らしくなる。

▶ because 以下は、because they A (would not brake ...), B (could be routed ...), and C (could travel ...). と、述部が 3 つ並列する形になっている。

▶ 文全体を通して、動詞に would や could がついた仮定法過去が使われている。「仮に自動運転の乗り物が現実になったら」という〈仮定〉の意味が含まれている。

2 【as many as ～】【even so】

(l.29) Some urban areas have **as many as** 3.5 parking spaces per car; **even so**, people looking for parking account for 30% of total driving time in urban business districts.

▶ as many as ～は、数詞の前に置かれて「～ほども多くの（= no fewer than ～）」の意味。数の多さを強調する表現で、可算名詞に対して使われる。

▶ even so は、前述の内容を受け「（確かにそれは事実ではあるが）そうは言っても、それにもかかわらず（= nevertheless）」の意味を表す。

▶ people 以下は、「都市部の商業地域では、人々は駐車場探しに総運転時間の 30%を費やしている」の意味。the time spent by people looking for parking accounts for 30% of total driving time ...、あるいは the process of people looking for parking accounts for 30% of total driving time ... と同意。

3 【文構造】【come to *do*】【関係代名詞 that】【sit + C】

(l.36) But in a future without drivers, people will **come to wonder** why they tolerated such a high rate of road deaths, and why they spent so much money on machines **that** mostly **sat unused**.

▶ 全体の構文は、..., people will come to wonder A (why they tolerated ... road deaths), and B (why they spent ... sat unused).「人々は A と B を不思議に思うようになるだろう」。並列した why に導かれる 2 つの名詞節が wonder の目的語。

▶ come to *do*「～するようになる」

▶ that mostly 以下は、machines を先行詞とする関係代名詞節。

▶ sat unused の sit は「（物が）～の状態のままである」の意味で、S sit C の形で使われ、C には形容詞、分詞などがくる。ここでは過去分詞 unused が置かれ、sit unused「使われないままで置かれている」の意味。

4 【sound】【consider O to be ～】【不定詞の完了形】

(l.38) A world of self-driving vehicles may **sound odd**, but coming generations will probably **consider** the era of car ownership **to have been** much stranger.

▶ S may sound odd は SVC の文型で、「S は奇妙に聞こえる［思える］かもしれない」。

▶ consider O to be ～は「O が～であると考える［見なす］」。to have been と完了形の不定詞になっているのは、「車を所有していた時代が自動運転車の世界より以前のことだった」ことを表している。

46

展開	段落	要旨
導入	1	将来、完全に（①　　　　　　　　）走行の車が現実となる可能性がかなり高い。
本論①	2	（②　　　　　　　）運転の電動ポッドを利用すれば、自動運転車の未来を体感できるだろう。
本論②	3	自動運転車は、交通事故の原因の大半を占める（③　　　　　　　　　　）を犯さないため、交通事故の（④　　　　　　　）頻度は激減するはずだ。
本論③	4	自動運転車は交通の流れをより（⑤　　　　　　　）にする。それらは、急ブレーキをかけず、最適なルート選択をし、互いに接近して進めるので、道路容量の増加につながる。また、搭乗者は運転中に他のことができるので、大幅な（⑥　　　　　　　　）の向上が見込める。
本論④	5	自動運転車が常に走っていれば、必要な（⑦　　　　　　　）スペースはずっと少なくなる。無駄な（⑦　　　　　　　）スペースの開放は、都市部の居住スペースを増加させる。同時に、自動運転は労働者の（⑧　　　　　　　　）通勤も可能にするだろう。
結論	6	将来の人々は、車を所有していた今の時代を奇妙に感じるだろう。

■　以下を参考にして、「段落要旨」の下線部分を中心にまとめてみよう。
▶「導入」の内容に「本論②〜④」までの内容をまとめてつなげると書きやすい。
【記述例】：「完全な自動運転車が現実となれば「本論②」「本論③」「本論④」など多くのことが期待できる」
▶「本論②〜④」の内容は全て名詞化して字数を稼ぐ。
【言い換え例】「激減する→減少」、「円滑にする→円滑化」、「可能にする→容易化」など。

（下書き）

10　　　　　　　　　　　　　　　　　　20

10　　　　　　　　　　　　　　　　　　20

Advances in technology over the past 200 years have been remarkable and have ⏳24 brought us many benefits. However, the integration of technology into society has not always been smooth. The first industrial revolution began in Britain in the late 18th century. Machines developed at the time could make clothes much more efficiently,

5 easily, and cheaply than before. Even so, not everyone felt happy about (1)this at first. Groups of skilled weavers and textile machine operators, known as Luddites, feared that their jobs would be taken away. They began a labor movement in order to protest and resist the widespread use of the new technology by factory owners. Their protest actions included destroying machines — crimes for which some Luddites were killed

10 by authorities.

As we now know, these technological advances did not slow down. Over time, ⏳25 they became widely accepted and appreciated. Before long, other innovations like the steam engine were powering heavy machinery across Europe and beyond. The second industrial revolution, toward the end of the 1800s, brought the gasoline engine and the

15 use of electricity. The third industrial revolution, in the late 20th century, produced computers as well as digital technologies and communications. And, recently, experts have declared that developments in artificial intelligence (AI) and advanced robotics have led us into the fourth industrial revolution.

Even today, however, we hear warnings about (2)the potentially harmful effects of ⏳26

20 contemporary technologies. Some observers claim that the latest AI inventions could have negative impacts on workers, businesses, and society as a whole. The main concern, as in past eras, is that machines will replace humans in the workplace. These observers suggest that a large number of occupations might be lost to AI and robots in the next few years. Taxi and truck drivers, cleaners, and factory workers are among

25 those considered to be at risk.

The fear is even expressed that the AI revolution might lead to mass unemployment. ⏳27 According to some experts, up to 800 million jobs could be lost globally by 2030. Moreover, the workers who will lose their jobs to machines are likely to be those with fewer skills and less education, increasing the gap between rich and poor. Some people

30 believe that this will create social conflict and instability.

However, we do not necessarily need to take such a negative outlook on the future. ⏳28 While some job losses due to AI-powered technologies will occur, there will not be an overall decrease in employment. New jobs will appear, and humans will always be needed to supervise and maintain the robots. And there are many jobs which machines

35 just cannot do, such as those involving social relationships and interpersonal skills.

For instance, a machine would have trouble replacing a friendly salesperson, or a kind and compassionate care giver. Indeed, in a recent report for the Organization for Economic Cooperation and Development, (3)researchers predicted that not as many jobs will disappear as had previously been thought.

🕮29   So how can we make the smoothest possible transition into the new era that the fourth industrial revolution has brought? It is important to recognize and respond to the impacts of technological inventions on people's lives. Governments must provide retraining and new opportunities for those workers who lose their jobs. Also, when many jobs disappear in specific regions, it will be necessary to bring new high-tech industry to those towns and cities.

🕮30   People experienced fears of being displaced by machines during previous industrial revolutions. However, the new technologies actually created new employment opportunities and ended up enhancing our lives significantly. Keeping in mind both the conflicts and the successes of the past, let's cooperate today in creating the best shape for our AI-powered future together.

1
....
....

2　　第一次産業革命 （　　　　　）　　　第二次産業革命 （　　　　　）
　　　　第三次産業革命 （　　　　　）　　　第四次産業革命 （　　　　　）

3

4
....

5
....
....

6
....

7
....

| 語句 | 音声は、英語に続いて日本語の意味が読まれます。 | CD 2 - Tr 31 ～ 34 |

入試基本レベル

1 **remarkable** [rimάːrkəbl] _____

20 **claim** [kléim]（動）_____

22 **concern** [kənsə́ːrn]（名）_____

22 **replace** [ripléis] _____

26 **mass** [mǽs]（形）_____

28 **be likely to** *do* _____

34 **maintain** [meintéin] _____

44 **specific** [spəsífik] _____

48 **end up** *doing* _____

48 **keep ～ in mind** _____

入試標準レベル（共通テスト・私大）

4 **efficiently** [ifíʃəntli] _____

7 **protest** [prətést]（動）_____

8 **resist** [rizíst] _____

8 **widespread** [wáidspréd] _____

8 **protest action** _____

17 **advanced** [ədvǽnst]（形）_____

19 **warning** [wɔ́ːrniŋ] _____

19 **potentially** [pəténʃəli] _____

20 **contemporary** [kəntémpərèri]（形）_____

20 **observer** [əbzə́ːrvər] _____

21 **as a whole** _____

22 **era** [íːrə] _____

23 **occupation** [ὰkjəpéiʃən] _____

25 **at risk** _____

30 **conflict** [kάnflikt]（名）_____

31 **outlook** [áutlùk] _____

33 **overall** [óuvərɔ̀ːl]（形）_____

35 **involve** [inválv] _____

48 **significantly** [signífikəntli] _____

49 **cooperate** [kouάpərèit] _____

入試発展レベル（二次・有名私大）

2 **integration of A into B** _____

6 **textile** [tékstàil]（名）_____

10 **authorities** _____

12 **innovation** [ìnəvéiʃən] _____

13 **steam engine** _____

13 **power** [páuər]（動）_____

23 **be lost to A** _____

26 **unemployment** [ʌ̀nimplɔ́imənt] _____

30 **instability** [ìnstəbíləti] _____

34 **supervise** [súːpərvàiz] _____

37 **compassionate** [kəmpǽʃənət] _____

40 **transition** [trænzíʃən] _____

46 **displace** [displéis] _____

48 **enhance** [inhǽns] _____

その他

6 **weaver** [wíːvər] 織工

6 **Luddite** [lʌ́dait] ラッダイト

13 **heavy machinery** 重機械、重機

16 **communications** 情報技術、通信手段

17 **robotics** ロボット工学

35 **interpersonal** [ìntərpə́ːrsənəl] 対人（関係）の

37 **care giver** 介護士、看護者

43 **retraining** [riːtréiniŋ] 再教育、再訓練

1 【不定詞の副詞的用法〈目的〉】【名詞表現】

(l.7) They began a labor movement **in order to** protest and resist **the widespread use of the new technology by factory owners**.

▶ They は、前文（第1段落第6文）の Groups of skilled weavers ... known as Luddites を指す。
▶ in order to *do* は不定詞の副詞的用法のうち〈目的〉を明確に表して、「～するために」。ここでの in order to に続く動詞は、protest「抗議する」と resist「抵抗する」の2つ。
▶ the widespread use of the new technology by factory owners「工場主による新たな技術の広範な使用」は長い名詞表現。名詞表現は「形容詞＋名詞」を「動詞＋副詞」に直してみるとわかりやすいことがある。ここも "factory owners used the new technology widely" の名詞表現である。

2 【lose A to B】【be likely to *do*】【分詞構文】

(l.28) Moreover, (S)the workers who will **lose** their jobs **to** machines (V)are likely to be (C)those with fewer skills and less education, **increasing** the gap between rich and poor.

▶ Moreover は、前文の「最大8億の仕事が失われる」という内容を受けて、「（それに）加えて、さらに」の意味。
▶ 関係代名詞節 who will ... to machines は the workers を修飾している。those with fewer skills and less education で「技術をあまり持たない、教育水準の低い人々」という意味。
▶ lose their jobs to machines は「機械に自分たちの仕事を奪われる」。lose A to B で「A を B に奪われて失う、B のために A を奪われる」。第3段落第4文では、その受動態 be lost to ... の形で使われている。
▶ be likely to *do* は「～しそうである、～する可能性が高い」。
▶ increasing 以下は分詞構文。分詞 increasing の主語はコンマの前までの内容で、「機械に仕事を奪われる労働者は、おそらく～のような人々である可能性が高く、そのため貧富の格差が広がるだろう」の意味。... less education, and that will increase ... あるいは ... less education, which will increase ... と書き換え可能。

3 【possible の用法】【関係代名詞節】

(l.40) So how can we make **the smoothest possible** transition into the new era **that the fourth industrial revolution has brought**?

▶ make a smooth transition into ...「…に円滑に移行する」。the smoothest possible transition で「可能な限り円滑な移行」。この possible は最上級を強めて、「考えうる～の、可能な限り～の」という意味。
　　ex. What is the worst possible thing that could happen?
　　　　「起こりうる最悪の事態はどんなことだろう」
▶ that the fourth industrial revolution has brought は、the new era を先行詞とする関係代名詞節。

4 【分詞構文】【keep A in mind】【cooperate in *doing*】

(l.48) **Keeping in mind** both the conflicts and the successes of the past, let's **cooperate** today **in** creating the best shape for our AI-powered future together.

▶ Keeping ... past, は分詞構文。「…を念頭に置きながら、…を心に留めて」の意味。
▶ keep A in mind「A を念頭に置く、A を心に留める」。ここでは A に当たる both ... past が長いため、keep in mind A の語順になっている。
▶ cooperate in *doing*「～することに協力する」

段落要旨　各段落のまとめとなるように、空所に適切な語句を入れなさい。（同じ番号には、同じ語句が入ります）

展開	段落	要旨
導入	1	社会への科学技術の（①　　　　　）は常に順調だったわけではない。第一次産業革命の際、機械に職が奪われることを恐れた（②　　　　　）が工場主に対して労働運動を行った。
本論①	2	第二次産業革命はガソリンエンジンと（③　　　　　）の利用を、第三次産業革命はデジタル技術・情報技術とコンピューターをもたらした。現在、私たちは（④　　　　　）と先端ロボット工学の発達により第四次産業革命へと導かれている。
本論②	3	現代科学技術の潜在的な悪影響についての警告を今でも耳にする。主な懸念は過去の時代と同じく、仕事場で機械が人間に（⑤　　　　　）というものだ。
本論③	4	（④　　　　　）革命が世界的な（⑥　　　　　）を生み出すかもしれないという不安がある。貧富の差が拡大し、社会的対立や不安定が生まれると考える人々もいる。
本論④	5	将来に対して否定的な展望を持つ必要はない。いくつかの仕事がなくなる一方で、雇用の全般的な減少はないという予測もある。
本論⑤	6	第四次産業革命がもたらした新時代に可能な限り円滑に移行するには、（⑦　　　　　）が人々の生活に与える影響を認識し、それに対応することが重要だ。
結論	7	過去の対立と成功の両方を念頭に置いて、（④　　　　　）が原動力となる我々の未来に向けて協力しよう。

百字要約　「段落要旨」を参考にして、本文全体の内容を百字程度の日本語で要約しなさい。

（下書き）　　　　　　　　　　　　　　　10　　　　　　　　　　　　　　　20

（空欄の原稿用紙）

10　　　　　　　　　　　　　　　20

（空欄の原稿用紙）

Memo

CD 2
🔊 35

An ant rushes over a sandy beach on a path full of twists and turns. It turns right, left, back, then halts, and moves ahead again. How can we explain the complexity of the path it chose? We can think up a sophisticated program in the ant's brain that might explain its complex behavior, but we'll find that it does not work. What we have
5 overlooked in our efforts to speculate about the ant's brain is (1)the ant's environment. The structure of the wind-and-wave-molded beach, its little hills and valleys, and its obstacles shape the ant's path. The apparent complexity of the ant's behavior reflects the complexity of the ant's environment, rather than the ant's mind. The ant may be following a simple rule: get out of the sun and back to the nest as quickly as possible,
10 without wasting energy by climbing obstacles such as sand mountains and sticks. Complex behavior does not imply complex mental strategies.

A lone, hungry rat runs through what psychologists call a T-maze★. It can turn 🔊 36 either left or right. If it turns left, it will find food in eight out of ten cases; if it turns right, there will only be food in two out of ten cases. The amount of food it finds is
15 small, so it runs over and over again through the maze. Under a variety of experimental conditions, rats turn left most of the time, as one would expect. But sometimes they turn right, though (2)this is the worse option, puzzling many a researcher. According to the logical principle called (3)*maximizing*, the rat should always turn left, because there it can expect food 80 percent of the time. Sometimes, rats turn left in only
20 about 80 percent of the cases, and right 20 percent of the time. Their behavior is then called *probability matching*, because it reflects the 80/20 percent probabilities. It results, however, in a smaller amount of food; (4)the expectation is only 68 percent. The rat's behavior seems irrational. Has evolution miswired★ the brain of this poor animal? Or are rats simply stupid?

25 We can understand the rat's behavior once we look into its natural environment 🔊 37 rather than into its small brain. Under the natural conditions of foraging★, a rat competes with many other rats and animals for food. If all go to the spot that has the most food, each will get only a small share. The one mutant★ organism that sometimes chooses the second-best patch would face less competition, get more food, and so
30 be favored by natural selection. Thus, rats seem to rely on (5)a strategy that works in a competitive environment but doesn't fit the experimental situation, in which an individual is kept in social isolation.

The stories of the ant and the rat make (6)the same point. In order to understand 🔊 38 behavior, one needs to look not only into the brain or mind but also into the structure
35 of the physical and social environment.

* T-maze「T型迷路」　miswire「誤った造りにする」　foraging「エサをあさること」　mutant「突然変異の」

1 ....

....

2 ....

....

3 ....

4 If there are two possible ways, (a)(   )% of the rats turn left to go to a place where there is an (b)(   )% probability of finding food. In that case, the probability of finding food is 64%. In the same way, if 20% of the rats turn right to go to a place where there is a (c)(   )% probability of finding food, the probability of finding food is(d)(   )%. Thus, the expectation is 68%.

5 (ア) ....

....

(イ) ....

....

6 ....

....

語句	音声は、英語に続いて日本語の意味が読まれます。	CD 2 - Tr 39 ～ 42

入試基本レベル

4	**behavior** [bihéivjər]	
7	**apparent** [əpǽrənt]	
7	**reflect** [riflékt]	
10	**waste** [wéist] （動）	
21	**result in ~**	
27	**compete** [kəmpíːt]	
28	**share** [ʃéər] （名）	
30	**favor** [féivər] （動）	
30	**rely on ~**	
32	**individual** [ìndəvídʒuəl] （名）	
35	**physical** [fízikəl]	

入試標準レベル（共通テスト・私大）

1	**rush** [rʌ́ʃ] （動）	
1	**path** [pǽθ]	
2	**complexity** [kəmpléksəti]	
3	**think up ~**	
3	**sophisticated** [səfístikèitid]	
4	**complex** [kɑmpléks] （形）	
5	**overlook** [òuvərlúk]	
6	**structure** [strʌ́ktʃər] （名）	
9	**nest** [nést] （名）	
11	**imply** [implái]	

11	**strategy** [strǽtədʒi]	
12	**lone** [lóun]	
17	**option** [ɑ́pʃən]	
17	**puzzle** [pʌ́zl] （動）	
18	**logical** [lɑ́dʒikl]	
18	**principle** [prínsəpl]	
21	**probability** [prɑ̀bəbíləti]	
22	**expectation** [èkspektéiʃən]	
23	**evolution** [èvəlúːʃən]	
24	**stupid** [st(j)úːpid]	
28	**organism** [ɔ́ːrgənìzm]	
31	**competitive** [kəmpétətiv]	
32	**isolation** [àisəléiʃən]	

入試発展レベル（二次・有名私大）

2	**halt** [hɔ́ːlt] （動）	
5	**speculate** [spékjəlèit]	
7	**obstacle** [ɑ́bstəkl]	
23	**irrational** [irǽʃənl]	

その他

1	**twists and turns**	曲がりくねり
6	**wind-and-wave-molded**	風と波で形作られた
29	**patch** [pǽtʃ]	小さな土地、区画
30	**natural selection**	自然淘汰

本文解説

1 【関係代名詞 that】【think up】【基本動詞 work】

(l.3) We can **think up** a sophisticated program in the ant's brain **that** might explain its complex behavior, but we'll find that it does not **work**.

- ▶ that は関係代名詞で、先行詞は a sophisticated program「精巧なプログラム」。
- ▶ think up A / think A up は「A を思いつく、考え出す」（= devise）の意味。
- ▶ work は「機能する」の意味。it は、直接的には program を指すが、think up 以下 behavior までの「思いついた内容」を指すと考えてもよい。

2 【主語に条件が含まれる仮定法過去】

(l.28) The one mutant organism that sometimes chooses the second-best patch **would** face less competition, get more food, and so be favored by natural selection.

- ▶ 全体の構文は、The one mutant organism ... would face ..., get − , and so be favored 〜 . で、述語動詞が 3 つ並列されている。
- ▶ would は仮定法を表し、主語に仮定の条件が含まれている。「もし次善の場所を選ぶような突然変異的な生物がいたら、それは〜するだろう」= If one mutant organism sometimes chose the second-best patch, it would face ....
  - *eg.* A wise mother would be stricter with her children.
  「賢明な母親なら、もっと子どもに厳しくするだろう」

3 【関係代名詞 that】【前置詞＋関係代名詞】

(l.30) Thus, rats seem to rely on a strategy **that** works in a competitive environment but doesn't fit the experimental situation, **in which** an individual is kept in social isolation.

- ▶ that は関係代名詞で、先行詞は strategy「戦略」。but doesn't fit ... も関係代名詞節の続きである。
- ▶ in which の先行詞は the experimental situation で、〈an individual is kept in social isolation in the experimental situation〉となる。in which の前にコンマがあるが、明確な非制限用法というより、英文が長いのでコンマを付け加えたもので、制限用法に近い。

4 【接続詞の慣用表現 not only 〜 but also ...】【look into 〜】【brain vs. mind】

(l.33) In order to understand behavior, one needs to **look not only into** the **brain** or **mind but also into** the structure of the physical and social environment.

- ▶ 等位接続詞の慣用表現 not only A but also B の、A と B には同じ関係のものがくる。look into not only A but also B でもよいが、前置詞 into と続く名詞の関係を重視して、look not only into A but also into B となっている。
- ▶ look into 〜は「〜を調べる」（=investigate）の意味。
- ▶ brain は「脳」で、体の一部としての脳を指す。mind は「心、精神」が中心の意味だが、ここでは「頭脳、知性」（=intellect）の意味。

展開	段落	要旨
例示①	1	複雑なアリの行動は、アリの脳が精巧であるからではなく、アリの置かれた（①　　　　　　　）によるものである。複雑な行動が複雑な（②　　　　　　　）に直結するわけではない。
例示②	2	Ｔ型迷路の実験では、ラットはエサが見つかる可能性が高い方だけに行き続ければ、最も多くのエサを得ることができる。（＝「（③　　　　　　　）」）しかし、ラットは時としてエサが少ない方に行くという（④　　　　　　　）な行動をとることもある。（＝「確率対応」）
例示③	3	それは、ラットの置かれた自然（①　　　　　　）を調べれば理解できる。ラットの行動は、競争相手がいない方が有利だという戦略に基づいていると推測できるが、その戦略は競争がない実験の（①　　　　　　）には適していないのである。
結論	4	行動を理解するためには、脳や知性だけでなく、物理的、社会的（①　　　　　　　）も調べる必要がある。

（下書き）

CD 2
🔊43

Can you blame the scorching weather on climate change? Not really. Or at least not yet. In a National Oceanic and Atmospheric Administration* (NOAA) report released last week, researchers attempted to determine how much they could attribute six extreme weather events last year to human-caused global warming. Even now, months on, some
5　experts worry that drawing conclusions is too sudden. (1)Figuring out what caused a flood in Thailand or a drought in Texas is hard. Doing it quickly is harder.

🔊44

Scientists involved in NOAA's report thought that climate change did significantly increase the likelihood of last year's warm winter in the United Kingdom and heat wave in Texas, though their calculations are admittedly imperfect. Experts also determined
10　they could not show that global warming contributed to flooding in Thailand — the level of rainfall wasn't historically unusual.

🔊45

The conclusion? Anyone who, in the midst of a hurricane here or a heat wave there, simplistically blames greenhouse gas emissions is wrong. But it's also wrong to blame all extreme events on forces beyond human control.

🔊46

15　Repeated climate patterns such as El Niño and La Niña can influence extreme weather. But natural variability doesn't mean human activity hasn't been playing an increasing role in the formation of (2)extreme events, or in the scale of the resulting damage. Most obviously, more people are living in environmentally insecure zones. (3)Stripping land or degrading wetlands can leave humans more vulnerable to floods, as
20　in Thailand, or hurricanes, as in New Orleans.

🔊47

And the planet is certainly warming. Humans releasing heat-trapping gases into the atmosphere are almost certainly responsible for much, if not all, of that warming; the particular patterns of warming, comparison to the historical record, and the basic principles of physics all indicate this. On average, more energy in the system probably
25　increases the intensity or frequency of certain extreme weather events, such as very high temperatures, across the planet. Patterns emerge. In recent years, there have been more record-breaking heat events and fewer record-breaking cold ones. Scientists are also beginning — but only beginning — to assess how much particular incidents can be attributed to climate change in anything like real time.

🔊48

30　So, while (4)the science of attribution improves, what can you say the next time you're suffering from a sustained heat wave? This is the sort of thing that will get more common across a warming world. (5)That should be more than enough to spur Americans to demand action from their leaders.

* National Oceanic and Atmospheric Administration「アメリカの海洋大気庁」

❶
....
....

❷ ・..
・..
・..

❸
....
....

❹
....

❺
....

❻
....

| 語句 | 音声は、英語に続いて日本語の意味が読まれます。 | CD 2 - Tr 49 ～ 52 |

入試基本レベル

5	figure out ～	
7	be involved in ～	
15	influence [ínfluəns]（動）	
16	activity [æktívəti]	
18	obviously [ɑ́bviəsli]	
22	atmosphere [ǽtməsfìər]	
23	particular [pərtíkjələr]	
24	on average	

入試標準レベル（共通テスト・私大）

1	blame A on B	
3	attempt to *do*	
3	determine [ditə́:rmən]	
3	attribute A to B	
3	extreme [ikstrí:m]（形）	
5	draw a conclusion	
6	flood [flʌ́d]（名）	
7	significantly [signífikəntli]	
9	calculation [kæ̀lkjəléiʃən]	
9	admittedly [ədmítidli]	
10	contribute to ～	
13	emission [imíʃən]	
17	formation [fɔ:rméiʃən]	
17	scale [skéil]（名）	
19	strip [stríp]（動）	
22	if not all	
23	comparison [kəmpǽrəsn]	
24	principle [prínsəpl]	
24	physics [fíziks]	

24	indicate [índəkèit]	
24	system [sístəm]	（体）系、組織
25	intensity [inténsəti]	
25	frequency [frí:kwənsi]	
26	emerge [imə́:rdʒ]	
28	incident [ínsidənt]（名）	
29	anything like ～	
31	sustain [səstéin]	
33	demand A from B	

入試発展レベル（二次・有名私大）

6	drought [dráut]	
8	likelihood [láiklihùd]	
9	imperfect [impə́:rfikt]	
12	midst [mídst]	
14	beyond control	
18	insecure [ìnsikjúər]	
19	degrade [digréid]	
19	vulnerable to ～	
27	record-breaking	
28	assess [əsés]	
30	attribution [æ̀trəbjú:ʃən]	
32	spur A to *do*	

その他

1	scorching [skɔ́:rtʃiŋ]	焼け付くような
8	heat wave	熱波、酷暑
13	simplistically [simplístikli]	単純化して
16	natural variability	自然変動
21	heat-trapping gas	温室効果ガス

本文解説

1 【文構造】【間接疑問】【attribute A to B】

(l.2) In a National Oceanic and Atmospheric Administrationn (NOAA) report released last week, (S)**researchers** (V)**attempted** to (V')**determine** (O')**how much** they could **attribute** six extreme weather events last year **to** human-caused global warming.

▶ 全体の構造は、In a ... report, researchers attempted to determine ～「報告書で、科学者たちは～を確定しようとした」。

▶ determine の目的語は how 以下の間接疑問で、「どのくらい～できるのか確定する」。

▶ attribute A to B で「A を B のせいにする」。A が six extreme weather events last year「昨年の 6 件の極端な気候事象」、B が human-caused global warming「人間が引き起こした地球温暖化」。

2 【過去分詞の後置修飾】【助動詞 do】

(l.7) (S)**Scientists** involved in NOAA's report (V)**thought** that (S')**climate change** (V')**did significantly increase** (O')**the likelihood of last year's warm winter in the United Kingdom and heat wave in Texas**, though their calculations are admittedly imperfect.

▶ 全体の構造は、Scientists ... thought that ～．「…である科学者たちは～と考えた」。that 節内は climate change did ... increase the likelihood of ～「気候変動が～の可能性を実際に…高めた」。

▶ involved in NOAA's report は scientists を修飾し、「NOAA の報告書に関わった科学者たち」。

▶ 助動詞 did は動詞 increase を強調する用法で、「実際に」といった意味を動詞に付加する。

3 【文構造】

(l.16) But (S)**natural variability** (V)**doesn't mean** (O)**(that) human activity hasn't been playing an increasing role in the formation of extreme events, or in the scale of the resulting damage**.

▶ 全体の構造は、natural variability doesn't mean (that) ～「自然変動は～ということを意味しない」。SVO の文型。目的語となる節を導く that が省略されている。

▶ hasn't been playing an increasing role in the formation ..., or in the scales of ～「…の形成、あるいは～の規模において、さらなる役割を果たし続けていない」

4 【省略 if not all】【同格】

(l.21) (S)**Humans** releasing heat-trapping gases into the atmosphere (V)**are** almost certainly responsible for much, **if not all**, of that warming; (S)**the particular patterns of warming, comparison to the historical record, and the basic principles of physics all** (V)**indicate** this.

▶ if not all は (even) if they are not responsible for all of that warming の省略されたもの。「彼らが温暖化のすべてに責任があるわけではないとしても」

▶ セミコロン (;) 以下の主語は the particular patterns of warming, comparison to the historical record, and the basic principles of physics all まで。最初の 3 つの語句と all は同格。A, B, and C all「A、B それに C のすべてが～」 all は indicate を修飾する副詞ともとれる。

5 【more than enough】【spur A to *do*】

(l.32) That should be **more than enough** to **spur** Americans to demand action from their leaders.

▶ more than enough の直訳は「十分以上（なこと）」。

▶ spur A to *do* で「A に～するようせき立てる」。

▶ この英文は、この段落の第 1 文 what can you say ... の答えとなっている。

展開	段落	要旨
序論①	1	人間が引き起こした（①　　　　　　　　　　　）が、どの程度極端な（②　　　　　　　　　）事象の原因になったかを解明することは難しい。
序論②	2	異常気象の原因が（①　　　　　　　　　　）であると考えられるものもあるが、それを証明できないものもある。
本論①	3	極端な事象をすべて（③　　　　　　　　　　　）のせいにすることも、すべて人の手に負えない力のせいにすることも間違っている。
本論②	4	（④　　　　　　　　　　　　　）やラニーニャといった自然変動が極端な事象に影響を与えている可能性はあるが、人間の活動が影響を与えていないともいえない。
本論③	5	人間には（①　　　　　　　　　）に対する多くの責任があることはほぼ間違いなく、それは分析や（⑤　　　　　　　　）の原則によって明らかである。
結論	6	異常気象の原因が特定できるまでの間は、指導者たちに（①　　　　　　　　　　　）に対する行動を起こすよう求めてもいいのではないだろうか。

百字要約　　「段落要旨」を参考にして、本文全体の内容を百字程度の日本語で要約しなさい。

（下書き）

We are already aware that our every move online is tracked and analyzed. But you couldn't have known how much Facebook can learn about you from (1)the smallest of social interactions — a 'like'*.

Researchers from the University of Cambridge designed (2)a simple machine-learning system to predict Facebook users' personal information based solely on which pages they had liked.

"We were completely surprised by the accuracy of the predictions," says Michael Kosinski, lead researcher of the project. Kosinski and colleagues built the system by scanning likes for a sample of 58,000 volunteers, and matching them up with other profile details such as age, gender, and relationship status. They also matched up those likes with the results of personality and intelligence tests the volunteers had taken. The team then used their model to make predictions about other volunteers, based solely on their likes.

The system can distinguish between the profiles of black and white Facebook users, getting it right 95 percent of the time. It was also 90 percent accurate in separating males and females, Democrats and Republicans. Personality traits like openness and intelligence were also estimated based on likes, and were as accurate in some areas as a standard personality test designed for the task. Mixing what a user likes with many kinds of other data from their real-life activities could improve these predictions even more. Voting records, utility bills and marriage records are already being added to Facebook's database, where they are easier to analyze. Facebook recently partnered with offline data companies, which all collect this kind of information. (3)This move will allow even deeper insights into the behavior of the web users.

Sarah Downey, a lawyer and analyst with a privacy technology company, foresees insurers using the information gained by Facebook to help them identify risky customers, and perhaps charge them with higher fees. But there are potential benefits for users, too. Kosinski suggests that Facebook could end up as an online locker for your personal information, releasing your profiles at your command to help you with career planning.

Downey says the research is the first solid example of the kinds of insights that can be made through Facebook. "This study is a great example of how the little things you do online show so much about you," she says. "You might not remember liking things, but Facebook remembers and (4)it all adds up."

* a 'like': フェイスブック上で個人の好みを表示する機能。日本語版のフェイスブックでは「いいね！」と表記される。

1 ....

2 ·
....
....
·
....
·
....

3 ....

4 ....
....

5 ....

6 ....

語句 音声は、英語に続いて日本語の意味が読まれます。　　　　CD 2 - Tr 59 〜 62

入試基本レベル

4	**design** [dizáin]（動）	
10	**detail** [díːteil]（名）	
16	**male** [méil]（名）	
16	**female** [fíːmeil]（名）	
18	**mix A with B**	
23	**behavior** [bihéivjər]	
24	**lawyer** [lɔ́ːjər]	
25	**gain** [géin]（動）	
28	**release** [rilíːs]（動）	
32	**add up**	

入試標準レベル（共通テスト・私大）

1	**be aware that ～**	
1	**track** [træk]（動）	
1	**analyze** [ǽnəlàiz]	
5	**predict** [pridíkt]	
7	**accuracy** [ǽkjərəsi]	
7	**prediction** [pridíkʃən]	
8	**lead** [líːd]（形）	
8	**colleague** [káliːg]	
9	**scan** [skǽn]（動）	
9	**match A up with B**	
10	**gender** [dʒéndər]	
10	**relationship** [riléiʃənʃip]	
10	**status** [stéitəs]	
11	**personality** [pə̀ːrsənǽləti]	
11	**intelligence** [intélidʒəns]	
12	**model** [mádl]（名）	
14	**distinguish between A and B**	

15	**get A right**	A を正しく（理解）する
15	**accurate** [ǽkjərət]	
16	**trait** [tréit]	
17	**estimate** [éstəmèit]（動）	
18	**(be) designed for ～**	
23	**insight** [ínsàit]	
24	**analyst** [ǽnəlist]	
25	**identify** [aidéntəfài]	
26	**charge A with B**	
26	**fee** [fíː]	
27	**end up as ～**	
28	**at one's command**	
29	**solid** [sáləd]（形）	

入試発展レベル（二次・有名私大）

5	**solely** [sóulli]	
16	**Democrat** [déməkræt]	
16	**Republican** [ripʌ́blikn]	
21	**partner with ～**	
24	**foresee A doing**	
25	**insurer** [inʃú(ː)ərər]	

その他

3	**social interaction**	社会的交流
15	**～ percent of the time**	～％の確率で
16	**openness** [óupnnəs]	寛容さ
20	**voting record**	投票記録
20	**utility bill**	光熱費（の請求書）
21	**offline** [ɔ́(ː)fláin]（形）	オフラインの
28	**career planning**	キャリア計画

本文解説

1　【助動詞の完了形】【同格表現】

(l.1)　But you **couldn't have known** how much Facebook can learn about you from the smallest of social interactions — a 'like'.

> ▶ couldn't have *done* は「～したはずがない、～しなかったはずだ」の意味で仮定法過去完了の表現。この文の couldn't have known ～は「～ということまではおそらく知らなかったはずだ」ということ。

> ▶ the smallest の直後に、thing または unit といった語を補って考える。「social interactions の最も小さなもの［単位］」

> ▶ ダッシュ（—）に続く a 'like' は、the smallest of social interactions の内容を具体的に説明している同格表現。

2　【文構造】

(l.8)　(S)<u>**Kosinski and colleagues**</u> (V)<u>**built**</u> (O)<u>**the system**</u> by scanning likes for a sample of 58,000 volunteers, and matching them up with other profile details such as age, gender, and relationship status.

> ▶ 全体の構造は、Kosinski and colleagues built the system by ...「コジンスキ氏と同僚たちは…することによってシステムを作った」。

> ▶ 前置詞 by の目的語は、scanning ... と (and) matching ... の2つの動名詞句。「…を細かく調べて、それらを…と組み合わせることによって」

3　【主語になる動名詞】【mix A with B】

(l.18)　(S)<u>**Mixing**</u> what a user likes **with** many kinds of other data from their real-life activities (V)<u>could improve</u> (O)<u>these predictions</u> even more.

> ▶ 主部は Mixing ... activities までの動名詞句。主語が「人」ではないので、主語の部分を副詞的に訳すとよい。「…を組み合わせることは、～を向上させるだろう」→「…を組み合わせると、～は向上するだろう」

> ▶ mix A with B は「A を B と組み合わせる」。what で始まる関係代名詞節 what a user likes が A、B は「実際の生活の活動から得られた他の多くの種類のデータ」。

4　【文構造】【foresee A *doing*】【help A *do*】

(l.24)　(S)<u>**Sarah Downey, a lawyer and analyst with a privacy technology company**</u>, (V)<u>foresees</u> (O)<u>insurers</u> **using** the information gained by Facebook to **help them identify** risky customers, and perhaps **charge** them with higher fees.

> ▶ 主部は Sarah Downey, a lawyer and ... company まで。a lawyer 以下は、Sarah Downey を説明している同格表現。

> ▶ foresee A *doing*「A が～すると予見する」

> ▶ to help them identify ... and (parhaps) charge ～「彼らは…を特定し、～を請求するのを助ける」は、help A *do* の *do* が2つ（identify と charge）並列されている形。them は insurers を指している。

展開	段落	要旨
導入	1	フェイスブックの「（①　　　　　　　）」からどれほどあなたに関して知ることができるか、想像できなかっただろう。
本論①	2	研究者たちは、人々が好んだページ情報だけで（②　　　　　　　）を予測するシステムを作った。
本論②	3	サンプルの人々による「（①　　　　　　　）」と、彼らの（③　　　　　　　　　　）などを組み合わせてシステムを構築した。そのモデルを使い、別の人たちの「（①　　　　　　　）」だけをもとに、その人たちの（②　　　　　　）を予測した。
本論③	4	このシステムは、高確率で人種や支持政党を識別できるが、より多様なデータと組み合わせれば、予測はさらに向上するだろう。複数の（④　　　　　　　　　　）企業と提携し、情報収集を行っているフェイスブックは、ユーザーの行動をより深く考察できるだろう。
本論④	5	（⑤　　　　　　）会社はリスクのある顧客を特定するのにフェイスブックの情報を利用するかもしれない。一方利用者は、オンライン上に自身の情報を公開して（⑥　　　　　　）計画に役立てるかもしれない。
結論	6	ネット上で行うささいな行動が、多くの（②　　　　　　）につながる。自分が「（①　　　　　　　）」を表明したことは覚えていなくても、フェイスブックは覚えているのだ。

（下書き）　　　　　　　　　　　　　　　　　　　10　　　　　　　　　　　　　　　　　　20

CD 2
◎63

Have you heard the well-known claim that only 7 percent of any spoken message is based on verbal communication? So-called experts tell us that a full 93 percent of any message is communicated nonverbally. This contention is, of course, absolute rubbish.

◎64

The 7-percent formula is endorsed by many professional communication trainers. They tell us that of the 93 percent figure referring to nonverbal communication, 55 percent is through body language and the other 38 percent is through tone of voice.

◎65

I attended a communications workshop recently in which the facilitator* quite confidently emphasized (1)these statistics. I was, to put it indelicately, dumbfounded*. I challenged her by asking, "Do you mean that if I stood in front of this class and spoke in Chinese, as long as my body language and tone of voice were consistent with my message, you would all understand me?" She used all the communication skills at her command to virtually slap me down. She supported her claims by quoting the research done by the eminent psychology professor Albert Mehrabian.

◎66

(2)The rest of the class, impressed that this principle was being put forth as the result of a scientific study and not just as a myth or rumor, nodded in agreement. I acquiesced*, remaining unconvinced.

◎67

I consulted my friend Google and did some research. Yes, experiments were conducted by Albert Mehrabian, currently professor emeritus* of psychology at the University of California at Los Angeles. But (3)the research in question was done in 1967, using one word at a time to measure what the listener believed to be the feeling of the speaker and determine if the listener liked the speaker. The experiment was never intended to measure how well the listeners understood what the speaker was trying to communicate.

◎68

Mehrabian has published his work and findings in the book *Silent Messages*. On his website, Mehrabian states: "*Silent Messages* contains a detailed discussion of my findings on inconsistent messages of feelings and attitudes (and the relative importance of words vs. nonverbal cues)." I found that the professor says (4)his findings have been misquoted. Max Atkinson, a communications researcher in Wells, Somerset, United Kingdom, quoted from a personal e-mail he received from Mehrabian; in the e-mail, Mehrabian said:

◎69

"I am obviously uncomfortable about misquotes of my work. From the very beginning, I have tried to give people the correct limitations of my findings. Unfortunately, the field of self-styled 'corporate image consultants' or 'leadership consultants' has numerous practitioners with very little psychological expertise."

◎70

I learned an important lesson from that workshop I attended. (5)I learned not to swallow what some people call "facts" without careful examination of how the so-called facts were obtained, especially the ones that on the surface seem unnatural.

* facilitator「司会者」 dumbfounded「あぜんとした」 acquiesce「黙従する」 professor emeritus「名誉教授」

❶ ....

....

❷ ....

....

❸

❹ ....

❺ ....

....

❻ ....

| 語句 | 音声は、英語に続いて日本語の意味が読まれます。 | CD 2 - Tr 71 〜 74 |

入試基本レベル

1	**claim** [kléim]（名）	
5	**figure** [fígjər]（名）	
5	**refer to** 〜	
14	**impress** [imprés]（動）	
18	**currently** [ká:rəntli]	
25	**contain** [kəntéin]	
26	**relative** [rélətiv]（形）	

入試標準レベル（共通テスト・私大）

2	**verbal** [vá:rbl]	
2	**so-called** [sóukɔ́:ld]	
3	**nonverbally** [nànvá:rbəli]	
3	**absolute** [ǽbsəlù:t]（形）	
6	**tone** [tóun]（名）	
8	**emphasize** [émfəsàiz]	
8	**statistics** [stətístiks]	
10	**consistent** [kənsístənt]	
11	**at** *one's* **command**	
12	**virtually** [vá:rtʃuəli]	
14	**principle** [prínsəpl]	
15	**myth** [míθ]	
17	**consult** [kənsʌ́lt]	
18	**conduct** [kəndʌ́kt]（動）	
21	**determine** [ditá:rmin]	
22	**intend O to** *do*	
25	**detailed** [dí:teild]	

32	**limitation** [lìmitéiʃən]	
34	**numerous** [n(j)ú:mərəs]	
36	**swallow** [swɑ́lou]（動）	
37	**obtain** [əbtéin]	
37	**on the surface**	

入試発展レベル（二次・有名私大）

3	**contention** [kənténʃən]	
3	**rubbish** [rʌ́biʃ]（名）	
4	**formula** [fɔ́:rmjələ]	
12	**quote** [kwóut]（動）	
13	**eminent** [éminənt]	
15	**rumor** [rú:mər]	
16	**unconvinced** [ʌ̀nkənvínst]	
26	**inconsistent** [ìnkənsístənt]	
27	**cue** [kjú:]（名）	
28	**misquote** [mìskóut]	

その他

4	**endorse** [endɔ́:rs]	支持する
8	**put it indelicately**	下品な言い方をすれば
9	**challenge** [tʃǽlindʒ]（動）	異議を唱える
12	**slap down** 〜	批判する、こきおろす
14	**put forth** 〜	発表する、公表する
33	**self-styled** [sélfstáild]	自称の
34	**practitioner** [præktíʃənər]	専門職従事者
34	**expertise** [èkspə:rtí:z]	専門的知識

本文解説

1 【仮定法過去】【接続詞 as long as】

(l.9) Do you mean that **if** I stood in front of this class and spoke in Chinese, **as long as** my body language and tone of voice were consistent with my message, you **would** all understand me?

▶ 全体の構文は、Do you mean that ...?「あなたは…だと言うのですか?」。that 節内は if I stood ~ , as long as ..., you would all understand me「もし私が立ったとしたら、…である限り、あなたはすべて理解するだろう(と)」。

▶ if I stood ~ , you would ... の 典型的な仮定法過去「もし立ったとしたら、理解するだろう」の形。なお、仮定法は時制の一致を受けないので、次のように間接話法で表現しても時制は変わらない。

    cf. I asked her if she meant that if I stood in front of that class and spoke in Chinese, ..., they would all understand me.

▶ as long as ~ は「~する限り」の意。my body language and tone of voice were consistent with my message は「私のボディーランゲージと声の調子が私の伝えたいことと一致している」。

2 【分詞構文】【進行形の受動態】

(l.14) The rest of the class, **impressed** that this principle **was being put** forth as the result of a scientific study and not just as a myth or rumor, nodded in agreement.

▶ 全体の構文は、The rest of the class ... nodded in agreement.「クラスの残りの人たちは同意してうなずいた」の、SV の文型。

▶ impressed that ... は付帯状況を表す分詞構文で、「…ということに感銘を受けて」。

▶ the principle was being put forth は進行形の受動態で、「この原理が発表されている」。

3 【分詞構文】【関係代名詞 what】【in question】

(l.19) But the research **in question** was done in 1967, **using** one word at a time to measure **what** the listener believed to be the feeling of the speaker and determine if the listener liked the speaker.

▶ 全体の構文は、the research in question was done in 1967「問題の研究は 1967 年に行われた」で、using 以下はその研究の具体的な内容。using one word at a time to measure ~ and determine ...「1 回に 1 つの単語を用いて~を測り、…を決定した」

▶ what the listener believed to be the feeling of the speaker「聞き手が話し手の感情だと確信したもの」believe O to be ~「O が~だと信じる」の O の部分に相当するのが関係代名詞 what。

▶ the speaker は言葉を発した人、the listener はその言葉を聞いた人。ともに被験者。

4 【前置詞 on】

(l.25) *Silent Messages* contains a detailed discussion of my findings **on** inconsistent messages of feelings and attitudes (and the relative importance of words vs. nonverbal cues).

▶ 全体の構文は、*Silent Messages* contains a detailed discussion「『サイレント・メッセージ』は詳細な議論を含んでいる」。

▶ 前置詞 on は「~に関する」。about より正式で、「(専門的な内容)に関して」。

▶ inconsistent messages of feelings and attitudes とは、「(言葉とは)一致しない、感情や態度の伝えるもの」。

▶ カッコ内は、この本の中で扱われている他の内容を付け加えたもの。

展開	段落	要旨
序論①	1	語られたメッセージの 7% だけが（①　　　　　　　）による伝達で、残りの 93% は（②　　　　　　　）による伝達だ、というでたらめな主張がある。
序論②	2	その 93% の内訳は、55% が（③　　　　　　　　）、38% が声の調子によるものであるという。
本論①	3	ある講習会で、司会者がこの統計を強調していたので、筆者は反論した。しかし、司会者は（④　　　　　　　　）という著名な心理学教授の研究結果を持ち出して、自説を裏付けた。
本論②	4	講習会に参加した人々は、この主張が科学的な研究結果をもとにして発表されていることに感銘を受けた。
本論③	5	その主張の根拠になっている実験は、感情の伝達に焦点を置いたものであり、聞き手が話し手の伝える内容をどれだけ（⑤　　　　　　　）したかを評価するものではなかった。
本論④	6	（④　　　　　　　　）は、自身の著書である『サイレント・メッセージ』から、誤った（⑥　　　　　　　）がなされていると述べている。
本論⑤	7	彼は、誤った（⑥　　　　　　　）に対して不快に感じている。
結論	8	私は、特定の人々が「（⑦　　　　　　　）」と呼び、主張しているものを、その背景を入念に調べることなくうのみにしてはならない、ということを学んだ。

百字要約　　「段落要旨」を参考にして、本文全体の内容を百字程度の日本語で要約しなさい。

（下書き）

CD 2

Since the start of the modern planet-hunting era more than 15 years ago, scientists ⊚75 have said their search wasn't about astronomy; it was about biology. These planet hunters are looking for earth-like life on distant worlds. That means the planets would have to be like ours too. They'd have to be about the same size. They'd have to have
5 the same rocky core. (1)They'd also have to travel around their parent stars at just the right distance to have liquid water, the main ingredient for life. Scientists call this the habitable zone.

But while the big discovery hasn't been made yet, researchers might be getting ⊚76 close. At a recent conference in Wyoming, a team of European scientists announced
10 the discovery of at least 50 new worlds. One of them, called (2)Goldilocks, circles a star about 36 light-years away in the constellation Vela★. The planet sits just inside its sun's habitable zone, though it is four times closer to its sun than the Earth is to ours. "It's a beautiful detection," says Geoff Marcy, who leads a different team of planet hunters at the University of California, Berkeley. "And it could possibly be habitable."

15 (3)Possible is the best anyone can say for now. A clearer answer will have to wait for ⊚77 more powerful telescopes to be built. If the answer turns out to be yes, the question of whether Goldilocks actually is home to life will depend on (4)many factors. To start with, does it have any water? Does it have a solid, rocky surface on which life can live? Does it have a cooling cloud layer to avoid overheating from its sun?

20 Nobody knows. It would be an unlikely bit of luck if the newly discovered world did ⊚78 have all (5)the right stuff for life. After all, so many conditions must be present. The newly discovered world is still a big deal, though. It proves that astronomers now have the technology to find these kinds of planets.

Most of the big planet announcements over the past two years have come from the ⊚79
25 Kepler space mission. The Kepler mission uses a high-powered orbiting telescope to search a section of the Milky Way galaxy★ for earth-like planets. In particular, it is used to study regular decreases in the brightness of stars. These tiny decreases in brightness are created by planets passing in front of their stars as they orbit.

The 50 new planets announced in Wyoming were discovered from the ground with ⊚80
30 a device called the High Accuracy Radial velocity Planet Searcher, or HARPS. HARPS uses a telescope at the European Southern Observatory in Chile to look for a star's slight (6)wobble. A wobble is a small change in a star's position as a planet travels around it. Wobbles occur when the gravity of an orbiting planet pulls the star one way, then the other. The very first "exoplanets" — planets that orbit distant stars other than
35 our sun — were found this way.

With so many unanswered questions, it's still a long shot that Goldilocks will turn ⊚81 out to be the first known exoplanet to support life. Even so, its discovery shows how far planet hunting has come. (7)With all of the searches going on worldwide, and with increasingly powerful technologies, it's just the beginning in what could be a series of
40 extraordinary discoveries that add further evidence to support the notion that humans are not alone in the universe.

★ constellation Vela「帆座（ほざ）」 the Milky Way galaxy「銀河系宇宙」

1
....
....

2
....
....
....

3
....

4
・ ....
・ ....
・ ....

5
....

6
....

7
....
....

8
....

語句　音声は、英語に続いて日本語の意味が読まれます。　　　　　**CD 2 - Tr 82 〜 85**

入試基本レベル

3	**distant** [dístənt]	
16	**turn out (to be)** ～	
17	**factor** [fǽktər]	
18	**surface** [sə́:rfəs] （名）	
19	**avoid** [əvɔ́id]	
20	**unlikely** [ʌnláikli]	
21	**condition** [kəndíʃən] （名）	
22	**prove** [prúːv]	
24	**announcement** [ənáunsmənt]	
26	**search A for B**	
27	**regular** [régjələr]	
27	**tiny** [táini]	
32	**slight** [sláit] （形）	
33	**occur** [əkə́:r]	

入試標準レベル（共通テスト・私大）

1	**era** [íərə]	
2	**astronomy** [əstrá:nəmi]	
2	**biology** [baiɑ́lədʒi]	
5	**core** [kɔ́:r] （名）	

6	**liquid** [líkwid]	
6	**ingredient** [ingrí:diənt]	
9	**conference** [ká:nfərəns]	
10	**circle** [sə́:rkl] （動）	
11	**sit** [sít]	存在する
13	**detection** [ditékʃən]	
17	**to start with**	
18	**solid** [sá:ləd] （形）	
19	**layer** [léiər]	
21	**stuff** [stʌ́f] （名）	
21	**present** [préznt] （形）	
22	**a big deal**	大変なこと、重大事
27	**brightness** [bráitnəs]	
30	**device** [diváis]	
33	**gravity** [grǽvəti]	
39	**a series of** ～	
40	**extraordinary** [ikstrɔ́:rdənèri]	
40	**evidence** [évədəns]	
40	**notion** [nóuʃən]	
41	**universe** [jú:nəvə̀:rs]	

入試発展レベル（二次・有名私大）

7　habitable [hǽbətəbl]

11　light-year

19　overheat [òuvərhíːt]（動）

28　orbit [ɔ́ːrbət]（動）

その他

1　planet-hunting　　惑星探査

3　earth-like　　地球に似た

5　parent star　　主星、親星

17　be home to ～　　～が存在する

19　cooling [kúːliŋ]（形）　　冷却する

20　a bit of luck　　1つの幸運

25　orbiting telescope　　軌道望遠鏡

30　the High Accuracy Radial velocity Planet Searcher
　　高精度視線速度系外惑星探査装置

31　the European Southern Observatory
　　ヨーロッパ南天天文台

32　wobble [wábl]（名）　　揺れ、ふらつき

34　exoplanet [éksouplæ̀nət]　　太陽系外惑星

36　a long shot　　あまり期待できないもの

本文解説

1　【文構造】【推量の would】【不定詞の形容詞的用法】【同格】

(l.5)　**They'd** also have to travel around their parent stars at just the right distance **to have** liquid water, **the main ingredient for life.**

▶ 全体の構造は「その惑星は主星の周りを回らなければならないだろう」。at 以下は travel around を修飾する副詞句で「～の距離で」。

▶ They は the planets を指し，They'd は前文と同じ They would の短縮形。この would は推量を表し「～だろう」という意味。

▶ to have ～は just the right distance を修飾する形容詞的用法の不定詞で、「～するための最適な距離」。

▶ , the main ingredient for life は同格表現で、liquid water を説明している。

2　【sit, sun の意味】【倍数表現】

(l.11)　The planet **sits** just inside **its sun's** habitable zone, though it is **four times closer** to its sun **than** the Earth is to ours.

▶ sit は「存在する、位置する」の意。

▶ its sun's は「the planet の太陽」、つまり the planet が周回している恒星のこと。sun には「（自ら発光していて、惑星の軌道の中心になる）恒星」の意味もある。

▶ 〈～ times ＋比較級＋ than A〉「A より～倍の…」　be close to ～「～に近い」

3　【turn out (to be) ～】【文構造】【同格の of】【名詞節を導く whether】

(l.16)　If the answer **turns out to be** yes, (S)**the question** of whether Goldilocks actually is home to life will depend on many factors.

▶ turn out (to be) ～「～であることがわかる」　　▶ 主節の主語は the question ～ life まで。

▶ the question of ～「～という疑問」の of は「同格」を表し、「～という、つまり」という意味になる。

▶ whether Goldilocks actually is home to life は名詞の役割をしていて、「ゴルディロックスが実際に～かどうかということ」。

4　【仮定法過去】【a bit of luck の意味】【助動詞 do】

(l.20)　It would be **an unlikely bit of luck** if the newly discovered world **did** have all the right stuff for life.

▶ 全体は仮定法過去で、「もし～だとしたら…だろう」。

▶ unlikely は「ありそうにない」。a bit of luck は「1つの幸運」。

▶ did は助動詞で、have を強調する表現。意味は「本当に持っている（としたら）」。

5 【前置詞 with】【形式主語】【a long shot の意味】

(l.36) **With** so many unanswered questions, **it's** still **a long shot that** Goldilocks will turn out to be the first known exoplanet to support life.

▶ with は理由を表し、「～があるので」。

▶ it は形式主語で、that 以下文末までが真主語。「～（that 以下）であることはまだ可能性が低い」という意味になる。a long shot はくだけた表現で、「一か八かの賭け、見込みのないもの（人）」という意味。

段落要旨 各段落のまとめとなるように、空所に適切な語句を入れなさい。（同じ番号には、同じ語句が入ります）

展開	段落	要旨
序論	1	科学者たちは、遠く離れた惑星上に（①　　　　　　　）にいるような生命体を探している。
本論①	2	最近、恒星の（②　　　　　　　）ゾーン内にある（③　　　　　　　　　）という惑星が発見された。
本論②	3	その惑星に生命体が存在するかを判断するには、より高性能の（④　　　　　　）が必要だ。また、水や岩石核、雲の存在など多くの要因が必要となる。
本論③	4	発見された新惑星が、生命に必要な要素をすべて持っている可能性は低い。
本論④	5	近年数々の惑星を発見している（⑤　　　　　　　）宇宙探査は、恒星の輝度の減少を観察する軌道（④　　　　　　）を使用している。
本論⑤	6	50 の新惑星を発見した機器は、惑星の引力が恒星を引き寄せることで発生する「（⑥　　　　　　）」を探す望遠鏡を使用している。
結び	7	数多くの宇宙探査や科学技術の発達を考えれば、（③　　　　　　　　　）の発見は、（①　　　　　）外生命体の存在を証明することへの始まりにすぎない。

百字要約 「段落要旨」を参考にして、本文全体の内容を百字程度の日本語で要約しなさい。

（下書き）

10　　　　　　　　　　　　　　20

10　　　　　　　　　　　　　　20

CD 2

Think about all your important beliefs and ideas. They may relate to what you study, how you view yourself and others, your political viewpoints, and religious beliefs. Now ask yourself if you prefer to look for evidence that supports and strengthens those ideas, or do you like to look for evidence that might weaken or disprove them? According to social psychologists, we often look for ways to confirm our views, and often avoid attacking them.

Peter Wason first explored this almost sixty years ago in a classic experiment. He presented twenty-nine psychology undergraduates with three numbers: 2, 4, and 6. They were told that their goal was to figure out a particular rule that explained this series of numbers. The actual rule used was very simple: the second number had to be larger than the first number, and the third number had to be larger than the second one. To help them complete the task, the students were allowed to write down any series of three numbers and show them to the experimenter. Every time the numbers matched the rule, the experimenter would tell them it was a match, but wouldn't explain the reason. They could (1)do this as many times as they liked until they were sure that they had figured out the rule. At that point, they could write it down and show it to the experimenter. The students were told to continue testing series of numbers and writing down possible rules until they arrived at the correct one.

Despite the fact that the actual rule was very simple, only six out of the twenty-nine students correctly figured it out on their first attempt. The reason for this was that the students spent most of their time trying to positively test their first ideas. For example, some of the students started by guessing that the rule related to the use of even numbers. They would then *only* write examples that included even numbers until they had persuaded themselves that the rule could only be about those numbers. What they often didn't do, for example, was include odd numbers in order to (2)negatively test their first idea.

This way of thinking is known as *confirmation bias* and it tells us something very important about how we develop our views about the world. When we think about our beliefs, we all feel that the truth is the most important thing for us. However, we are also very powerfully influenced by the way our minds work, and we are often not aware of it. This does not just relate to our preferences for confirming our beliefs rather than disproving them. Social psychologists have also found other influences. For example, we often prefer to continue to believe something because it is useful or emotionally important to us in some way.

Universities try to address these tendencies by emphasizing the importance of skills like critical thinking and debating. (A), what can often happen is that we only critically examine new ideas or beliefs we disagree with. (3)There is also some evidence that debating can actually strengthen your original ideas and beliefs, rather than making you question them.

So what can we do to avoid the effects of confirmation bias? One solution is to push ourselves to improve our understanding of different viewpoints. One advantage of the university seminar system is that (4)students are free to attend the classes of many different professors. Try to find a professor that disagrees with the ideas that you have already been taught. In addition, try to carefully read books that you disagree with, and spend time talking to people that have different ideas from your own. And don't just talk to them, but train yourself to see the conversation through their eyes. You might feel that they are obviously wrong, but it is important to understand why they feel the same way towards your ideas. In addition, try to view changing your ideas as exciting and challenging, and not something uncomfortable, threatening, and negative. It is very difficult to avoid confirmation bias when you are on your own. It is almost impossible when you are with a group that all agrees with the same idea. The best place to shape your thinking is therefore somewhere in the messy, ever-changing space between opposing arguments.

1

2

3

4

5

6

| 語句 | 音声は、英語に続いて日本語の意味が読まれます。 | CD 2 - Tr 92 〜 95 |

入試基本レベル

1 **belief** [bilíːf] _____

1 **relate to** 〜 _____

2 **view** [vjúː]（動）_____

9 **figure out** _____

9 **particular** [pərtíkjələr] _____

10 **actual** [ǽktʃuəl]（形）_____

14 **match** [mǽtʃ]（動）_____

14 **match** [mǽtʃ]（名）_____

18 **correct** [kərékt]（形）_____

19 **despite** 〜 _____

21 **positively** [pázitivli] _____

22 **guess** [gés]（動）_____

24 **persuade** [pərswéid] _____

25 **negatively** [négətivli] _____

30 **influence** [ínfluəns]（動）_____

44 **in addition** _____

47 **obviously** [ábviəsli] _____

49 **negative** [négətiv]（形）_____

53 **argument** [áːrɡjəmənt] _____

入試標準レベル（共通テスト・私大）

2 **political** [pəlítikəl] _____

2 **religious** [rilídʒəs] _____

3 **evidence** [évid(ə)ns]（名）_____

3 **strengthen** [stréŋkθn] _____

4 **weaken** [wíːkən] _____

5 **confirm** [kənfáːrm] _____

7 **explore** [iksplɔ́ːr] _____

7 **classic** [klǽsik]（形）_____

8 **present A with B** _____

8 **undergraduate** [ʌ̀ndərɡrǽdʒuet]（名）_____

10 **(a) series of** 〜 _____

20 **attempt** [ətémpt]（名）_____

23 **even number** _____

25 **odd number** _____

30 **be aware of** 〜 _____

33 **emotionally** [imóuʃənəli] _____

35 **emphasize** [émfəsàiz] _____

40 **solution** [səlúːʃən] _____

50 **on** *one's* **own** _____

53 **opposing** [əpóuziŋ] _____

入試発展レベル（二次・有名私大）

2 **viewpoint** [vjúːpɔ̀int] _____

4 **disprove** [disprúːv] _____

31 **preference for** 〜 _____

35 **address** [ədrés]（動）_____

36 **critical thinking** _____

41 **push O to** *do* _____

49 **challenging** [tʃǽlindʒiŋ] _____

49 **threatening** [θrétniŋ] _____

52 **messy** [mési] _____

その他

13 **experimenter** [ikspérəmèntər]

実験者

27 **confirmation bias** 確証バイアス

52 **ever-changing** 絶えず変化する

1 【間接疑問】【語彙】

(l.3) Now **ask yourself if you prefer** to look for evidence that supports and strengthens those ideas, or **do you like to look** for evidence that might weaken or disprove them?

▶ Now は文頭に置かれ、話の切り出し、話題の転換などに使われることがある。「さて、そこで」といった意味。
▶ ask yourself if ... は命令文の形で、「…かどうか自分に問いかけなさい」。if 以下には間接疑問の形がくる。直接疑問では "do you prefer to look for ... ?" と、主語と動詞の倒置が起こるが、間接疑問の中では〈S + V〉の語順のままで、倒置は起こらない。
▶ or 以下は直接疑問文になっているが、内容的には ask yourself の続きなので、or if you like to look for evidence that might weaken or disprove them と間接疑問の形で読み替えてかまわない。
▶ 〈名詞詞 + en〉、〈形容詞 + en〉で他動詞になる語がある。strength「強さ」→ strengthen「強化する」、weak「弱い」→ weaken「弱める」 *ex.* heighten「高くする」 darken「暗くする」

2 【every time：接続詞的用法】【would の用法】

(l.13) **Every time** the numbers matched the rule, the experimenter **would** tell them it was a match, but **wouldn't** explain the reason.

▶ 〈every time S + V〉で「S が V するたびに」。every time は接続詞的に使われている。
▶ would tell them の would、wouldn't explain の would は、どちらも過去の動作の〈反復〉、すなわち過去に何度も繰り返された行為を表している。否定形 wouldn't は「どうしても〜しようとしなかった」と強い〈拒絶・固執〉を表すことがあるが、ここにはそこまでの意味合いはないだろう。実験者が「法則に合った答えを持ってくる学生に『合っている』と言う、でも理由は言わない」という行動を、ずっと繰り返し続けたことを描写している。
▶ but の後ろには、主語 the experimenter が省略されている。
▶ the reason は、the reason why it was a match の意味。

3 【同格の that】【out of 〜】【figure it out：他動詞＋代名詞＋副詞】

(l.19) Despite the fact **that** the actual rule was very simple, only six **out of** the twenty-nine students correctly **figured it out** on their first attempt.

▶ despite は前置詞で「〜にもかかわらず」。in spite of 〜 と同意。
▶ that 以下は同格節を導き、the fact の内容を示している。the fact that ... で「…という事実」。
▶ out of は 2 語からなる群前置詞で、ここでは「〜（ある数）の中から」の意味で使われている。only six out of the twenty-nine students で「29 人の学生のうちたった 6 人」の意味。
▶ figure out は「（答えなどを）見つけ出す」という意味で、〈他動詞＋副詞〉からなる頻出イディオムの 1 つ。〈他動詞＋副詞〉の句動詞の目的語が代名詞の場合には、本例の figure it out や pick them up「彼らを車で迎えに行く」のように〈他動詞＋代名詞＋副詞〉の語順となる。

4 【文構造】【関係代名詞】【persuade *oneself* that ...】

(l.23) (S)They (V)would then *only* write (O)examples **that** included even numbers until they had **persuaded themselves that** the rule could only be about those numbers.

▶ 全体の構造は、They would write examples 〜 until ... .「彼らは…するまで〜の例だけを書き続けた」。
▶ that included even numbers は、examples を先行詞とする関係代名詞節。
▶ persuade *oneself* that ...「…だと自分を納得させる」→「…だと納得する［確信する］」

段落要旨　各段落のまとめとなるように、空所に適切な語句を入れなさい。（同じ番号には、同じ語句が入ります）

展開	段落	要旨
導入	1	社会心理学者によれば、私たちは自分の考えや信念を（①　　　　　）証拠を探すことが多く、それらを攻撃することはしばしば避ける。
本論①	2	（②　　　　　　　　　）は有名な実験により初めてこのことを調べた。（②　　　　　　　　）は学生たちに 3 つの数字を示し、それらを説明する法則を見つけ出すよう言った。
本論②	3	法則は非常に単純だったが、一部の学生しか最初の試みで正しく答えられなかった。これは、大半の学生が最初の考えを（③　　　　　）に確かめることにほとんどの時間を費やしたためだ。
本論③	4	この考え方は「（④　　　　　　　）」と呼ばれる。私たちは真実が最も重要だと感じているが、実際には（⑤　　　　）に大変強く影響されている。
本論④	5	大学は批判的思考や（⑥　　　　　）を重視することで、（④　　　　　）に対処しようとしている。だが、実際にはそれらがうまく機能していないことがある。
本論⑤	6	（④　　　　　　　）の影響を避けるには、異なった見方への理解を向上させるよう努めることだ。そして、自分の考えを変えることを前向きに捉えるべきだ。思考の形成には、正反対の議論に囲まれることが必要だ。

百字要約　「段落要旨」を参考にして、本文全体の内容を百字程度の日本語で要約しなさい。

（下書き）　　　　　　　　　　　　　　　　　　10　　　　　　　　　　　　　　　　　　20

（空欄の原稿用紙）

10　　　　　　　　　　　　　　　　　　20

（空欄の原稿用紙）

Memo

Vocabulary Building Drill

語句確認ドリル

【設問形式について】
◆ 空欄と選択肢があるもの　⇒　適語選択
◆ 問題文に下線があるもの　⇒　下線部と同意のものを選択
◆ （　）内に語句があるもの　⇒　正しい英文に並べかえ
◆ その他はカッコ内の指示に従いなさい。

Chapter 1

1. (a) to get rid of, or do away with something completely　((a) の意味を持ち、かつ空所に適した語)
   (b) The woman decided to (　) high-calorie food from her diet.
   ① cancel　　　② control　　　③ eliminate　　　④ organize　　　(近畿大)

2. The teacher told us to (　) the outcome of the experiment.
   ① make　　　② conduct　　　③ carry　　　④ predict　　　(中央大)

3. (a) to come into view or become known　((a) の意味を持ち、かつ空所に適した語)
   (b) The police believe the truth will always (　) after an investigation.
   ① decline　　　② emerge　　　③ foresee　　　④ suppose　　　(近畿大)

4. The marketing (　) was a big success because sales increased by 50%.
   ① storage　　　② respect　　　③ serve　　　④ strategy　　　(青森公立大)

5. His behavior is not (　) with his words.
   ① complex　　　② conservative　　　③ consistent　　　④ crossed　　　(鹿児島大)

6. The examiner handed out a test paper to each candidate.
   ① completed　　　② distributed　　　③ documented　　　④ reduced　　　(東京理科大・改)

Chapter 2

1. I have a lot of things to work (　) tonight.
   ① on　　　② by　　　③ up　　　④ to　　　(流通科学大)

2. We had to (　) how much money we spent each day in order to have enough left for our ticket home.
   ① convince　　　② limit　　　③ spread　　　④ waste　　　(宮城学院女子大)

3. Their family (　) are close, and they try to see each other as often as they can.
   ① bands　　　② bounds　　　③ binds　　　④ bonds　　　(亜細亜大)

4. (a) to be able to say who someone is, or what something is　((a) の意味を持ち、かつ空所に適した語)
   (b) She could (　) which person was her mother in the picture.
   ① comment　　　② estimate　　　③ identify　　　④ state　　　(近畿大)

5. Don't make you feel (　) over something you have no control of.
   ① guilty　　　② grateful　　　③ innocent　　　④ present　　　(大阪電気通信大)

6. When I began to study French at college, I (　) by my pronunciation.
   ① was tiring　　② was embarrassing　　③ was embarrassed　　④ was troublesome　(関西学院大)

Chapter 3

1. Tom is a good salesman. He knows how to <u>deal with</u> the customers.
    ①　handle　　　　　②　make fools of　③　shake hands with　　　　　　　　　（大阪電気通信大）

2. (a)　a person in your family who lived a long time ago　((a) の意味を持ち、かつ空所に適した語)
    (b)　Jean learned that her (　　) was a famous French artist.
    ①　ancestor　　　②　connection　　　③　generation　　　④　household　　　（近畿大）

3. In England most people support the football team (　　) the town or city of their birth.
    ①　constructing　②　defeating　　③　praising　　　④　representing　　　（法政大）

4. Spanish is the (　　) language of most Spaniards.
    ①　mother　　　②　birth　　　　③　natural　　　④　native　　　　（鹿児島大）

5. Most people believe that friendships usually (　　) over time.
    ①　cooperate　　②　evolve　　　③　invest　　　④　live　　　　（立命館大）

6. I (　　) a note of regret in his voice and saw that he was not happy.
    ①　absorbed　　②　detected　　③　excluded　　④　inhabited　　　（中央大）

Chapter 4

1. Please don't make (　　) of him because he speaks too slowly.
    ①　sure　　　②　laugh　　　③　favor　　　④　fun　　　⑤　fan　　　（鹿児島大）

2. Earthquakes occur <u>frequently</u> in parts of Japan.
    ①　instantly　　②　spontaneously　③　annually　　④　often　　　（玉川大）

3. (a)　a part of the body that can be tightened and loosened to make the body move
    (b)　Nancy hurt a (　　) in her leg while playing tennis.
    　　((a) の意味を持ち、かつ空所に適した語)
    ①　bone　　　②　knee　　　③　muscle　　　④　nerve　　　（近畿大）

4. We can't make any sandwiches because we've (　　) bread.
    ①　got through　②　gone out with　③　run out of　④　carried through　（杏林大）

5. Bill was trapped on a deserted island for three years, but he didn't (　　) to death because there were plenty of coconuts.
    ①　dream　　　②　starve　　　③　wander　　　④　absorb　　　（秋田県立大）

6. The <u>primary</u> cause of his failure is his illness.
    ①　main　　　②　pointless　　③　strange　　　　　　　　　　　　（大阪電気通信大）

Vocabulary Building Drill

語句確認ドリル

【設問形式について】
◆ 空欄と選択肢があるもの　⇒　適語選択
◆ 問題文に下線があるもの　⇒　下線部と同意のものを選択
◆ （ ）内に語句があるもの　⇒　正しい英文に並べかえ
◆ その他はカッコ内の指示に従いなさい。

Chapter 5

1. While I stood at the station, a girl (　　) me. (ふさわしくない語を選ぶ)
   ① approached　② attacked　③ recognized　④ spoke　⑤ waved at　(早稲田大)

2. We need to examine the electric power plant quite soon.
   The electric power plant should be (　　) as soon as possible. (同意文完成)
   ① escaped　② inspected　③ trained　④ possessed　(相模女子大)

3. This picture reminds me (　　) my childhood.
   ① at　② for　③ of　④ though　⑤ with　(九州産業大)

4. It's important to (　　) children for the little steps they take toward their goals.
   ① lead　② praise　③ punish　④ teach　(中央大)

5. Be careful not to lose your temper.
   ① forget　② get angry　③ remember　④ become ill　⑤ get cold　(中京大)

6. His performance was brilliant.
   ① active　② boring　③ excellent　④ popular　⑤ slow　(中京大)

Chapter 6

1. He is about to give a speech in English. As it's his first time in front of a big audience, he feels rather (　　).
   ① free　② obvious　③ nervous　④ elderly　(麗澤大)

2. That publishing company has the (　　) rights to sell the book in this country.
   ① exclusive　② excessive　③ expressive　④ extreme　(成城大)

3. (　　) the high cost, so many cities want to host international events like the Olympics because of the expected effect on tourism and local businesses.
   ① Though　② In spite　③ Despite　④ For　(東洋大)

4. She (　　) that she was planning to become a cabin attendant.
   ① refused　② prevailed　③ required　④ revealed　(大阪経済大)

5. My skating is showing some (　　).
   ① improvement　② total　③ necessity　④ decrease　(工学院大)

6. When something terrible happens, which results in death, destruction, and suffering, we call it a (　　).
   ① feature　② traffic　③ government　④ disaster　(亜細亜大)

Chapter 7

1. Social distancing is <u>the norm</u> in the natural world.
   ① irregular ② standard ③ guideline ④ abstract （北里大・改）

2. The driverless cars are fitted with radar systems and cameras to <u>detect</u> their surroundings.
   ① recognize ② permit ③ improve ④ modify （甲南大・改）

3. That publishing company has the (　　) rights to sell the book in this country.
   ① exclusive ② excessive ③ expressive ④ extreme （成城大）

4. Illness (　　) the prime minister to resign.
   ① forced ② forwarded ③ made ④ was prevented （杏林大・改）

5. Tom won't allow Kate (　　) the computer.
   ① use ② using ③ has used ④ to use （愛知大）

6. People will be judging you <u>based on</u> the way you give a speech.
   ① in spite of ② in place of ③ on the grounds of ④ regardless of （甲南大・改）

Chapter 8

1. My mother always <u>gives in to</u> my little sister too easily.
   ① argues with ② praises ③ scolds ④ surrenders to （日本大）

2. She engaged (　　) protecting the natural environment.
   ① to ② in ③ off ④ onto （亜細亜大）

3. Are you (　　) the risks you are going to take? （名古屋学院大）
   ① aware of ② obvious about ③ notable about ④ informative about

4. He was sleepy, so he drank some coffee to keep himself awake and (　　).
   ① alert ② customary ③ ethnic ④ appropriate （北里大）

5. Many people make the wrong (　　) that poverty is found only in the Third World.
   ① assumption ② definition ③ result ④ translation （拓殖大）

6. Her contribution deserves more (　　).
   ① shot ② loan ③ recognition ④ endurance （広島修道大）

Vocabulary Building Drill

語句確認ドリル

【設問形式について】
◆ 空欄と選択肢があるもの　⇒ 適語選択
◆ 問題文に下線があるもの　⇒ 下線部と同意のものを選択
◆ （　）内に語句があるもの　⇒ 正しい英文に並べかえ
◆ その他はカッコ内の指示に従いなさい。

Chapter 9

1. One barrier to world peace is the nuclear arms issue.
   ① place　　　② end　　　③ contribution　　　④ obstacle　　　（長崎大）

2. After the movie finished, there were no more buses, so I (A) walking (B) home.
   (A)　① ended up　② hadn't been　③ must have　④ needed
   (B)　① all the way　② at least　③ for a bit　④ to a degree　　（京都産業大）

3. Our program always places the highest (　　) on the health, safety and security of our students.
   ① premier　　　② premise　　　③ primary　　　④ priority　　（立教大）

4. The other day, a salesman tried to (　) me to buy a new computer.
   ① retreat　　② listen　　③ persuade　　④ applaud　　⑤ disagree　（中央大）

5. The hospital has seen an increase in patients (　) sore throats recently.
   ① falling behind　② measuring up　③ looking at　④ complaining of　（獨協大）

6. We really didn't want to report the incident to the police, but there was no (　).
   ① alternative　　② incentive　　③ initiative　　④ motive　　（立命館大）

Chapter 10

1. Japan's first artificial satellite was launched from Kagoshima.
   ① natural　　② international　　③ empty　　④ manmade　　（秋田県立大）

2. I added all of my favorite (　) to the soup.
   ① contracts　　② ingredients　　③ protests　　④ surfaces　　（立命館大）

3. I am looking for a (　) substance which removes stains.
   ① chemical　　② chemist　　③ chemistry　　④ medical　　（杏林大）

4. He often exaggerates his experiences when he talks to his sons about his younger days.
   ① explains　　② overstates　　③ persuades　　④ persists　　（日本大）

5. You should always be cautious when you buy a new house.
   ① careful　　② aggressive　　③ tricky　　④ emotional　　（中央大）

6. 次の定義にあてはまる語を選びなさい。
   someone who buys and uses products and services
   ① consumer　　② humidity　　③ bookkeeper　　④ dairy　　（東京都市大）

Chapter 11

1. The final (   ) of this train is Tokyo Station.
    ① destine   ② destiny   ③ destination   ④ destitute   ⑤ destruction （中央大）

2. Such high taxes are the moral (   ) of theft.
    ① equivalent   ② intimate   ③ legal   ④ summit   （東京理科大）

3. (a) to change from one vehicle to another （(a) の意味を持ち、かつ空所に適した語）
    (b) In order to get to the university, you have to take a No. 15 bus and then (   ) to a No. 21 bus.
    ① transfer   ② transform   ③ translate   ④ transport   （近畿大）

4. Special cars are allowed to move on <u>dedicated</u> roadways above the street.
    ① memorial   ② committed   ③ common   ④ exclusive   （法政大）

5. Parking <u>accounts for</u> as much as 24% of the area of American cities.
    ① explains   ② makes up   ③ saves   ④ finishes off   （法政大）

6. Car-lovers will regret the <u>passing</u> of machines that became symbols of personal freedom.
    ① movement   ② end   ③ approval   ④ advance   （法政大）

Chapter 12

1. A : I heard you bought a new car.
    B : Yes, I did. But I thought my new car would get better gas (   ).
    ① economy   ② effect   ③ efficiency   ④ running   （名古屋市立大・改）

2. You have to write your name, address and (   ) in the blanks below.
    ① application   ② discrimination   ③ occupation   ④ prescription （学習院大）

3. It is the tendency of older people to keep a distance from <u>contemporary</u> fashion.
    ① convenient   ② time-consuming   ③ comfortable   ④ modern   （日本大）

4. Wars often start because of a (   ) between countries or groups over territory.
    ① conflict   ② relief   ③ surrender   ④ void   （亜細亜大）

5. The traditional method <u>gave way to</u> an innovative one.
    ① started to use   ② let go
    ③ was changed by   ④ was replaced by   （東海大）

6. Please be (   ) about what you want for your birthday. Tell me exactly what you would like.
    ① narrow   ② obvious   ③ essential   ④ specific   （南山大）

Vocabulary Building Drill

語句確認ドリル

Chapter 13

1. It's easy to <u>speculate</u> about the past; the real challenge is to solve the problem you face right now.
　① achieve　　② forget　　③ remember　　④ research　　⑤ think　　（中央大）

2. evolution:　The development of plants, animals, etc. over a long period of time from simple forms to more （　） ones.
　① complex　　② fluent　　③ prudent　　④ simultaneous　　（東京理科大）

3. In attempting to describe how <u>sophisticated</u> chimpanzee intelligence is, some people mistakenly compare it to the intelligence of a five-year-old human child.
　① complex and advanced　　② full of brain cells
　③ limited in storage capacity　　④ rich in language ability　　（甲南大）

4. I can afford the new tax, but I refuse to pay it, as a matter of （　）.
　① contrast　　② invention　　③ principle　　④ suspicion　　（立命館大）

5. (a)　to suggest something without saying so directly　((a) の意味を持ち、かつ空所に適した語)
　(b)　I did not mean to （　） that it was your fault.
　① associate　　② engage　　③ imply　　④ relate　　（近畿大）

6. (a)　We had to compete behind the scenes with one of the biggest companies in Europe for the building project.　（中央大）
　(b)　The selection for this year's scholarships was highly （　）.
　((a) に含まれるいずれかの語の派生語)　_____

Chapter 14

1. Some people （　） this to violent comics and video games.
　① accuse　　② assume　　③ attribute　　④ blame　　（東邦大）

2. I have to （　） this math problem in five minutes.
　① go on　　② care for　　③ figure out　　④ look after　　（城西大）

3. （　） left a large area of the nation parched, with an extremely high risk of fire.　（桜美林大）
　① Severe drought　　② Frequent floods　　③ A heavy snowfall　　④ Large landslides

4. The citizen judges help （　） the guilt or innocence of the accused in criminal trials.
　① concentrate　　② determine　　③ persecute　　④ represent　　（東邦大）

5. We would like to thank everyone who has （　） to the project.
　① conducted　　② completed　　③ contributed　　④ confused　　（北海道医療大）

6. The hands on a clock <u>indicate</u> the time of day.
　① hide　　② swing　　③ fill　　④ show　　（東海大）

1. This paper (   ) the present conditions of the automobile market.
   ① amazes   ② analyzes   ③ prepares   ④ prescribes   (南山大)

2. Accurate is that which is (   ).
   ① full of mistakes   ② off the mark   ③ made together   ④ without error   (上智大)

3. My (   ) upstairs devised our department's financial plan.
   ① colleague   ② edition   ③ license   ④ port   (立命館大)

4. He didn't describe what had happened in (   ); he only told me the most important facts.
   ① detail   ② difference   ③ large   ④ smallness   (山梨大)

5. The risk involved was greater than the (   ) gain.
   ① committed   ② internal   ③ potential   ④ satisfied   (立命館大)

6. After trying on a dozen skirts, Helen ended (   ) not buying one at the store.
   ① from   ② off   ③ down   ④ up   (学習院大・改)

Chapter 16

1. (a) The total reaches an amazing (f   ).   (大阪歯科大)
   (b) Avoiding excess fat will help you maintain a good (f   ).
   (共通する 1 語)

2. Since you have prepared well, you'll feel (   ) when you have an interview.
   ① blank   ② confident   ③ negative   ④ subtle   (立命館大)

3. You cannot <u>emphasize</u> the point too much.
   ① stress   ② abbreviate   ③ eliminate   ④ locate   (中央大)

4. (a) always in the same way; regularly   ((a) の意味を持ち、かつ空所に適した語)
   (b) Mary (   ) got high grades; she never got less than an "A" in any of her subjects.
   ① consistently   ② deliberately   ③ occasionally   ④ rarely   (近畿大)

5. A person who has a good (   ) of English can get a good post at a major company.
   ① reason   ② behavior   ③ command   ④ sensation   (西南学院大)

6. Why do some companies test cosmetics by (   ) experiments on animals?
   ① conducting   ② proceeding   ③ carrying   ④ taking   (南山大)

Chapter 17

1. Something that is not solid and that you can pour easily. The most common (　　) is water.
　① blend　　　　② drip　　　　③ gas　　　　④ liquid　　　（近畿大）

2. Unemployment is a major (　　) in youth crime.
　① answer　　　② factor　　　③ failure　　　④ purpose　　（南山大）

3. Why do you think he was lying to you? Because he (　　) making eye-contact with me.
　① avoided　　　② tried　　　③ promised　　　④ cleared　（北海学園大）

4. The <u>terms</u> of payment were clearly listed at the bottom of the page.
　① conditions　② environments　③ deadlines　④ dates　　（玉川大）

5. Kevin liked all his classes, but he enjoyed his music class in (　　).
　① detail　　　② general　　　③ particular　　④ focus　（大阪学院大）

6. (　　) is anything you see or read that causes you to believe that something is true.
　① Persistence　② Innocence　③ Evidence　④ Insistence　（慶應義塾大）

Chapter 18

1. 下の Hint を参考に、空所内の頭文字から始まる単語を書き入れなさい。
　Did you find any (e　　　　　　) that this drug works on patients with diabetes?
　(Hint：proof, support for)　　　　　　　　　　　　　　　　　　（日本大）

2. Please (　　) your appointment before you go to the dentist.
　① advise　　　② blend　　　③ confirm　　　④ spare　（立命館大）

3. I tried to read the sign, but I couldn't (　　).
　① call it off　② figure it out　③ put it on　④ set it up　（武庫川女子大）

4. (a)　to make someone agree to do something by giving reasons why they should
　(b)　The wife tried to (　　) her husband to go to the hospital.
　　　((a) の意味を持ち、かつ空所に適した語)
　① claim　　　② maintain　　③ persist　　④ persuade　（近畿大）

5. There is a large movement against <u>discrimination</u> on the basis of race in that country.
　① corruption　② justice　　③ bias　　④ equality　（会津大）

6. She didn't look at the painting for very long. It was (　　) that she didn't like it.
　① essential　② obvious　③ crucial　④ substantial　（立命館大）

Cutting Edge Blue
Navi Book

カッティングエッジ・ブルー
ナビブック 〔付録〕

検印欄

1	2	3	4	5	6
7	8	9	10	11	12
13	14	15	16	17	18

年　　　　組　　　　番　氏名